OUT OF COMFORT, INTO CALLING

A 40-DAY JOURNEY FROM BEING TO BECOMING

Jodie Shannon

Out of Comfort, Into Calling
© **2025 Jodie Shannon**
All rights reserved.

Published in the United States by:
The Heart Helper
Atlanta, Georgia
WWW.THEHEARTHELPER.COM

ISBN (Hardcover): 979-8-218-74927-9
ISBN (Paperback): 979-8-218-70598-5

This book is a work of personal testimony, reflection, and inspiration. While it includes spiritual guidance, it is not intended as a substitute for professional counseling, therapy, or pastoral care.

Scripture Acknowledgments

Scripture quotations are taken from the following translations and are used by permission where applicable:

To those becoming.

Introduction

Oxford Languages defines *calling* as "loud cries or shouts of an animal" or "a strong urge toward a particular way of life or career." I define *calling* as the soft whisper God places in our hearts—one we spend a lifetime trying to speak out loud.

As spirit beings navigating this human experience, our duty is to share that God-given whisper with the world. The whispers are loud when we are young. Everyone is born with it, but as we grow older and continue to ignore it—delaying the fulfillment of our calling—it grows quieter and quieter. If we don't listen, the whisper eventually stops speaking and moves on to the next heart with enough courage to fulfill it.

I've come to realize that fulfilling a calling takes courage. Many are content with wondering, wishing, and dreaming about the call—rather than actually answering it.

The calling is already there. You feel it. You know it. The question is: **What are you going to do with it?**

Many don't fulfill their calling because they're comfortable with *being* and unwilling to put in the effort to *become*. According to *Psychology Today*, a staggering 92% of people never fulfill their dreams. That means only 8% turn dreams into reality. It saddens me to know that only 8% are answering the call. This means the majority are living minimal lives, even though God intended for all of us to be monumental.

Ignoring the call is a disservice to yourself. It leads to a path of lesser living because you can never be truly happy being only half the person you were destined to become. Many remain basic simply because they lack the boldness required to become what they truly desire. You might be one of these people—and I know that's hard to hear. I was once one of them, too.

The phone is ringing. Let this book be your reminder: **It's time to answer the call.**

Pick up the phone! God has been calling you for a very long time. You may have ignored the call, put Him on hold and never returned, or even changed your number just to avoid hearing from Him again. But what are you so afraid of? Failure should be the least of your worries. What you should be concerned about is *Judgment Day*, when you will be held accountable for not answering. And by then, it will be too late.

Pursuing your purpose may feel uncomfortable, but know this: you are not alone. God is walking with you—guiding you toward the destination He designed just for you.

It's time to move **out of comfort** and **into calling**.

This book will help you answer the call. Over the next 40 days, you'll transition from simply *being* to fully *becoming* if you commit to the simple biblical principles within. The goal is for you to begin seeing yourself the way God sees you, to recognize your purpose, to assess your God-given gifts, and to apply spiritual tools to help manifest your dreams.

If you want to be part of the 8% who make their dreams a reality, you must start listening to that whisper in your heart—and make a practical plan to shout it out to the world. Because those who fail to plan, plan to fail. This book is for the people who want to soar and fulfill their purpose.

The fact that you're reading this right now proves something powerful: You're ready. You're eager to be elevated. And I am proud of you for taking the first step.

I hope that this book provides you with the foundation for true success: a positive mind, a devoted heart, and a deep, unshakeable relationship with God.

Cheers to all of you who will walk boldly in your calling after reading this book.

TABLE OF CONTENTS

A Prayer for Purpose   1

The Biblical Significance of the Number 40   3

Day 1: You Cannot Shine If You Do Not Recognize You Are a Light   8

Day 2: Stop Depending on Sight When God Gave You Vision   13

Day 3: You Can Achieve It—If You're Willing to Work for It   17

Day 4: What You're Seeking Is Already Within You   20

Day 5: Give Yourself Grace Through Growth   23

Day 6: You Are an Ambassador for God   26

Day 7: You Are a Sacred Space   31

Day 8: Your Faith Will Turn It in Your Favor   35

Day 9: You're Built to Endure—Not Just to Survive   38

Day 10: You Have Access to Abundant Peace   43

Day 11: Self-Care Is the Start, Service Is the Assignment   46

Day 12: When You Are Disciplined, You Cannot Be Deterred   50

Day 13: Put Down the Vices to Pick Up the Victory   54

Day 14: Worrying Takes Away from Your Worth   59

Day 15: You Are an Ocean—Stop Seeking Validation from Streams   62

Day 16: Because of Your Faith, It Will Happen   65

Day 17: You Are a High-Value Being   68

Day 18: You Are Becoming   72

Day 19: You Win When You Function More in Spirit Than Self   76

Day 20: Just Because You Are in War Doesn't Mean You Won't
Win   80

Day 21: You Weren't Called to One Flower—You Were Given a
Garden   84

Day 22: Rereading the Old Chapters in Your Book Is Only Preventing
You from Writing New Ones   88

Day 23: Intuition Is a Whisper from God   92

Day 24: Your Path to God Doesn't Have to Be Difficult   96

Day 25: Reveal. Remove. Replace. Let God Do the Rearranging 100

Day 26: Choose to Inspire in a World That Influences   104

Day 27: The Wise Will Always Strive to Become Wiser. The Teacher
Will Forever Be a Student   108

Day 28: Sit in Silence with Yourself   112

Day 29: If You Don't Listen to the Screams of Your Heart, Your
Dreams Will Turn into Whispers   116

Day 30: Your Habits Have to Align with Your Calling   120

Day 31: Don't Let Praise Go to Your Head or Rejection Go to Your
Heart   125

Day 32: Your Inability to Forgive Is Keeping You from Becoming 130

Day 33: You Can Eat, but If You Are Not Hungry for God, You Will
Never Be Full   134

Day 34: Use Your Gift to Serve in Obedience to God   139

Day 35: Garnering Advice from the Wise Will Take You Higher   142

Day 36: Let Go So You Can Grow   145

Day 37: Your Assignment Will Be Revealed in Alignment   150

Day 38: Consistency Really Is Key   155

Day 39: Let Go of the Outcome   159

Day 40: You Can't Copy Someone Else's Calling   164

Biblical Figures Leaving Their Comfort Zones   169

A Prayer for Fulfillment   173

Don't Just Walk in the Calling—Keep It   175

A Prayer to Keep the Calling   178

A Prayer for Purpose

Heavenly Father,

I thank You for allowing me to journey through this human experience. I recognize that this life is a gift—one that many are not afforded—and I want to make the most of it while You still allow me to unwrap it.

Today, I come to You with a humble heart, acknowledging that I lack the courage I need to walk in my calling fully. I yearn for an unspeakable boldness—one that empowers me to step into Your will for my life. I no longer want to live in comfort if that comfort keeps me from the call You are asking me to answer. Order my steps, Lord, so that I walk in purpose each day. Let all of my interactions be divinely orchestrated. Connect me to the people who will support and uplift me as I fulfill the mission You have assigned to my life.

I'm praying for Your direction, and I surrender to You as the driver of my life. I empty myself so that I may be filled with You. I am ready to be Your instrument—play me as You see fit. Influence me in spirit so I may be an inspiration to others in the natural world. Let me use my gift to bring You glory—today and forevermore.

In Jesus' name,

Amen.

The Biblical Significance of the Number 40

The number 40 is referenced in the Bible over 150 times, which is indicative of its significance. So, what does the number 40 mean? Biblically, it represents periods of trial, tribulation, teaching, and testing—intended to prepare and transform the spirit being for radical spiritual growth.

Genesis 7:4 (NIV) states: *"Seven days from now, I will send rain on the earth for forty days and forty nights, and I will wipe from the face of the earth every living creature I have made."*

This 40-day period is symbolic of **cleansing**.

In the book of *Exodus*, we encounter Moses, a man given a divine calling he doesn't feel qualified for.

Exodus 3:10–11 (NIV) says: *"So now, go. I am sending you to Pharaoh to bring my people, the Israelites, out of Egypt." But Moses said to God, "Who am I that I should go to Pharaoh and bring the Israelites out of Egypt?"*

Moses doubted his ability and questioned whether he could truly be the answer.

How many of us have heard God call us, only to ignore the ringing? We fear the opposition, not realizing that opposition often paves the way for redemption. Moses learned to lean on God by spending time with Him and strengthening their relationship. Though initially apprehensive, Moses ultimately chose obedience.

Exodus 24:18 (NIV) tells us: *"Then Moses entered the cloud as he went up on the mountain. And he stayed on the mountain forty days and forty nights."*

This was a sacred time of communion and communication with God—essential for anyone seeking divine direction. We do not know our destination without God's guidance, and spending quality time with Him provides the direction we need.

After his time on Mount Sinai, Moses returned transformed.

Exodus 34:29 (NIV) states: *"When Moses came down from Mount Sinai with the two tablets of the covenant law in his hands, he was not aware that his face was radiant because he had spoken with the Lord."*

Spending time with God changes us spiritually, and that transformation becomes physically evident. When we dwell in

His presence, our internal light begins to shine outward. This 40-day period represents **communion** with God.

I don't know about you, but I've prayed for many things I wasn't prepared to receive—and I couldn't understand why God didn't answer. But in hindsight, I realize that unanswered prayers were actually divine protection. Had He answered them, I would've mishandled the blessing.

The Israelites experienced this as well. They were delivered from bondage, yet they could not enter the Promised Land because of their disobedience and ungratefulness. They spent their days complaining about what they didn't have rather than praising God for what He had already done.

As a result, they wandered in the wilderness for 40 years.

Numbers 14:33–34 (NIV) says: *"Your children will be shepherds here for forty years, suffering for your unfaithfulness, until the last of your bodies lies in the wilderness. For forty years—one year for each of the forty days you explored the land—you will suffer for your sins and know what it is like to have me against you."*

Disobedience has a cost. Sometimes, access to the promise is delayed because we haven't followed God's instructions. We must be purified before we are ready to receive what we've prayed for—or we will mishandle it. This 40-year period symbolizes **purging**.

Perhaps the most well-known example of the number 40 is found in the Gospels, where Jesus fasted for 40 days and 40 nights.

Matthew 4:2–4 (NIV) states: *"After fasting forty days and forty nights, he was hungry. The tempter came to him and said, 'If you are the Son of God, tell these stones to become bread.' Jesus answered, 'It is written: Man shall not live on bread alone, but on every word that comes from the mouth of God.'"*

In this passage, Jesus is tested by Satan, but more importantly, He is trained by God. He applies what He's been taught. He didn't just know the Word—He lived it. The Word wasn't just *on* Him—it was *in* Him.

God will continue to test us until we pass. Just like students can't advance to the next grade without first passing an exam, we can't step into the next level of our calling without passing the spiritual test. This 40-day period symbolizes **testing**.

If you really want to understand the significance of the number 40, imagine your life as a blank sheet of paper. Over the years you've written your own story, line by line. But when you surrender your life to God, He comes and gently erases every word—every mistake—and forgives you in Jesus' name. Then, He begins writing your story Himself. And let me tell you: He is the greatest storyteller of all time. If you give Him the pen, your life will become a bestseller.

So I ask you:

- Are you ready to let God be your **Author**?
- Are you ready to let Him be your **Teacher**?
- Your **Doctor**?
- Your **Guide**?

Over the next 40 days, if you shrink your ego, He will enlarge your spirit.

Transformation starts now.

Day 1: You Cannot Shine If You Do Not Recognize You Are a Light

Find your light.

You were born with a purpose, and that purpose is to do God's will. Purpose looks different for everyone, but one thing we all have in common is this: however your purpose manifests, you are meant to be a light in the world.

In the book of *Matthew*, Jesus refers to us as the *"salt of the earth."* Upon researching the context of this statement, I discovered that during the time in which the Bible was written, salt was used as a preservative for various foods, as refrigeration did not exist. According to *Merriam-Webster*, a preservative is defined as "an additive used to protect against decay, discoloration, or spoilage" and "having the power of preserving." To preserve is "to keep safe from injury, harm, or destruction."

You are meant to preserve souls, and everything you need to do so already resides within you. God is the electricity, the Holy Spirit is the switch, and you are the bulb. In order to shine, you must turn on the Spirit. You have to recognize that you are a light—because you are connected to the Spirit. If you do not tap into the Source, you will never have access to the power!

How can you be a light to the world if you don't recognize the light within yourself? The ability to shine is already inside you. You were born with it. But many never discover their light because they live in self and forget they are spirit.

You are a spiritual being brought into this human experience to bring life to a world that is dying daily. Your gift should bring good to the world and glory to God. That is how you preserve the people.

The world is in dire need, and you do not have time to play small. We serve a big God—and you've been blessed with the ability to walk into a room and light it up in Spirit.

Sugar may be sweet, but it's salt that saves. Stay connected to God, and help others connect to Him as well. **You are a light.** The world is already dark—it doesn't need you playing dim.

Matthew 5:13–16 (NLT) "*You are the salt of the earth. But what good is salt if it has lost its flavor? Can you make it salty again? It will be thrown out and trampled underfoot as worthless. You are the light of the world—like a city on a hilltop that cannot be* *hidden. No one lights a lamp and then puts it under a basket. Instead, a lamp is placed on a stand, where it gives light to everyone in the house. In the same way, let your good deeds shine out for all to see so that everyone will praise your heavenly Father."*

Ephesians 5:8 (NKJV) *"For you were once darkness, but now you are light in the Lord. Walk as children of light."*

How to Recognize Your Light:

- **See who you are without distractions.**

  When I stopped drinking, I was finally able to appreciate who I was—with a sober mind and an open heart. The Spirit could speak to me because I wasn't clouded by a vice. I spent time with myself, and I liked who I was—without needing alcohol to have fun, without always being on my phone, and without being consumed by the chaos of life.

I simply *was*, and that stillness helped me fall in love with me. You can't love what you don't know, and you can't shine gifts you haven't unpacked.

- **Identify what you're passionate about and proficient in.**

  What are you good at? What sets your soul on fire?

If you can answer these questions, you'll begin to discover where your light is meant to shine. I have a friend who *loves* being a teacher. When you see him with his students, it's evident—his passion and proficiency align. He shines through teaching because he's walking in his purpose. He is *salt* to the children he serves.

I, on the other hand, have never desired to be a teacher—and that's okay. That's not my calling. My light wouldn't shine in that realm. You have to find the right space to shine, one that aligns with both your passion and your proficiency.

To Do:

Take a piece of paper—or use your *Out of Comfort and Into Calling* journal—and for Day 1, write down:

- The things you love about yourself.
- The things you are passionate about.
- The things you are proficient at.

What are you naturally good at?

Circle one gift and brainstorm how you can use it to benefit others. Ask yourself: *How can God get glory from the thing I'm naturally good at?*

Day 2: Stop Depending on Sight When God Gave You Vision

Release your expectations and become engulfed in God's will over your wants.

Because of our human tendencies, it can be hard to believe we can achieve what we can't plainly see. We often treat our desires as distant dreams—potentially attainable but unlikely. The human perspective is rooted in *sight*, but the divine perspective is anchored in *vision*. Thankfully, God gifted us with a spirit, and through the Spirit, we receive a vision.

Vision is God's will. Sight reflects our wants. Sight can be disappointing—but vision is **delightful, destined, and divine**.

Vision is a purposeful promise, and it's worth the wait because God knows exactly what we need. You may feel stuck right now because you're expecting God to answer prayers that, if granted, would bring you pain. But God desires to prosper you—not harm you.

It's time to release what you thought your life would look like—because what God has prepared for you is far greater than anything you've imagined.

Holding on to your version of the plan is hurting you. Let go of the wish. God has already assigned you *wealth*—spiritually, mentally, and physically. Vision requires trust in God and faith in the favor He's placed over your life.

Hebrews 11:1 (NIV) reminds us: *"Now faith is confidence in what we hope for and assurance about what we do not see."*

God will never give you a blessing prematurely. If you're not developed in spirit or character, the blessing could become a burden. Trust His will. Trust His perfect timing. It's time to get out of the driver's seat. Walk to the passenger side, sit down, and let the **more experienced driver—God—take the wheel.**

Scripture to Meditate On:

Habakkuk 2:3 (NLT) "This vision is for a future time. It describes the end, and it will be fulfilled. If it seems slow in coming, wait patiently, for it will surely take place. It will not be delayed."

Mark 9:23 (NIV) "'If you can'?" said Jesus. "Everything is possible for one who believes."

How to Focus on God's Vision:

- **Erase your expectations.** We've all envisioned the picture-perfect life—married by 30, thriving career by 32, picket fence and a dog. But life isn't a movie, and the script you've written may not be the one God wants you to star in. It's time to accept that your expectations may need to be erased. Expectations often lead to disappointment.

- **Listen more than you speak.** Shhh. You need to hush in order to hear. You can't hear God clearly when your own voice is louder than His. The Spirit works best in stillness, not when competing with your distractions or the megaphone of your mind.

To Do:

Go to God in prayer. Ask Him to help you release your expectations. The beliefs you've carried about what your life "should" be are heavy baggage. It's time to leave it behind.

- Write down who you thought you'd be.

- Bless that version of yourself, and let it go.

- Write a one-page letter of forgiveness to yourself for the version you didn't become.
- Now, promise yourself to become an instrument for God to use. Let Him mold you like clay into the image He intentionally designed.

Day 3: You Can Achieve It—If You're Willing to Work for It

You can't speak of faith and have no works. It's time to act.

There is no dream too big or too small. If God placed it in your heart, you *can* achieve it. The real question isn't whether you have the ability—it's whether you have the *discipline*.

Are you a dreamer but not a doer? Do you have a million-dollar mind with pennies in pursuit?

You were born rich in Spirit, but you're too afraid to spend your God-given wealth. That's why your pursuit of passion feels poor. You have the seeds—you just haven't planted them.

Those who labor will reap. Those who don't plant will go hungry. So, are you hungry enough? Praying is powerful—but it's not enough. **Faith without works is dead.** Give God something to bless. If you work, He'll pay your wages—and then some.

Scriptures to Meditate On:

Matthew 25:23 (NKJV) *"His lord said to him, 'Well done, good and faithful servant; you were faithful over a few things, I will* make you ruler over many things. Enter into the joy of your lord.'"

2 Timothy 2:6 (ESV) *"It is the hard-working farmer who ought to have the first share of the crops."*

Psalm 128:2 (ESV) *"You shall eat the fruit of the labor of your hands; you shall be blessed, and it shall be well with you."*

Proverbs 10:4 (NIV) *"Lazy hands make for poverty, but diligent hands bring wealth."*

Proverbs 13:4 (NIV) *"A sluggard's appetite is never filled, but the desires of the diligent are fully satisfied."*

Proverbs 20:4 (NIV) *"Sluggards do not plow in season, so at harvest time, they look but find nothing."*

How to Take Action:

- **Finish what you started.** You don't need a new idea. You need **discipline**, not distraction. The first idea God gave you was good enough—you just abandoned it too soon.
- **Break your cycle of laziness by changing your routine.** Respectfully, your dreams are suffering because you don't make time for them. I wrote this devotional at 11:51 PM

on a Monday—because I'm hungry for my destiny. You make time for everything else. Now, make time for your future.

To Do:

Go back to Day 1 and revisit the gift you circled.

- Research people in that field. What do you admire or dislike about their brand or business?
- What would your business or brand look like?
- Attend a conference, workshop, or networking event related to your passion.
- Take notes. Connect with like-minded people.

Then, take one step toward your dream. Start the website. File the LLC. Price the retail space. Design the book cover.

Be intentional with your dream and exceptional with your execution.

Day 4: What You're Seeking Is Already Within You

The love you desire has already been delivered. It lives inside you.

You are enough. Say it with me: *"I am enough."*

The world has a way of making us feel empty, but it's *you* who brings fullness. Self-love isn't trendy—it's divine. It's the fuel for faith and the foundation of calling.

The enemy wants you to dislike yourself so you'll forget that you're divine. When you forget your divinity, you invite destruction, distraction, and detours from your destiny.

You were born loved. So loved, in fact, that Jesus paid the cost *before* you even asked. You don't need to chase love when God has already chosen you.

Scriptures to Meditate On:

Psalm 139:13–14 (NIV) *"For you created my inmost being; you knit me together in my mother's womb. I praise you because I* *am fearfully and wonderfully made; your works are wonderful, I know that full well."*

Romans 8:37–39 (NIV) *"No, in all these things, we are more than conquerors through him who loved us. For I am convinced that neither death nor life, neither angels nor demons, neither the present nor the future, nor any powers, neither height nor depth nor anything else in all creation, will be able to separate us from the love of God that is in Christ Jesus our Lord."*

Mark 12:31 (NIV) *"The second is this: 'Love your neighbor as yourself.' There is no commandment greater than these."*

How to Be Love:

- **Do not look for love. Remember, you embody it.** When you seek love, it shrinks to a drop. When you embody love, it expands to an ocean.
- **Serve others.** Self-love isn't just spa days—it's service. Acts of service are a reflection of God's love. When you serve, you're being the church.

To Do:

- Volunteer somewhere this weekend.

- Find a way to serve—whether in your church, your community, or a local shelter.

Also:

- Meditate on verses that affirm God's love for you.
- Memorize them. Let them hug your heart. As your relationship with God deepens, you'll begin to experience His love—like a child finally appreciating a parent's sacrifices.

Day 5: Give Yourself Grace Through Growth

Changing seasons isn't bad. They're blessed.

We're so good at giving grace to others—but often forget to offer it to ourselves. Would you speak to a friend the way you speak to yourself?

Growth can be uncomfortable—even painful. But it's necessary. The human experience has no manual. We'll get lost. We'll feel pain. But suffering strengthens. Pain produces perseverance. Brokenness becomes a bridge to your breakthrough.

Even plants must be pruned to grow. If not, dead leaves begin to rot the root. So ask yourself: **What's rooting your root?** Is it fear? Anxiety? Depression? Trauma? It's time to grow. The Bible says you walk through the valley—not sit in it.

Get up. Grow.

Scriptures to Meditate On:

James 1:2–4 (NIV) *"Consider it pure joy, my brothers and sisters, whenever you face trials of many kinds because you know that the testing of your faith produces perseverance. Let* *perseverance finish its work so that you may be mature and complete, not lacking anything."*

Romans 5:3–5 (NIV*)** *"Not only so, but we also glory in our sufferings because we know that suffering produces perseverance; perseverance, character; and character, hope. And hope does not put us to shame because God's love has been poured out into our hearts through the Holy Spirit, who has been given to us."*

Hebrews 10:36 (NIV) *"You need to persevere so that when you have done the will of God, you will receive what he has promised."*

How to Accept Growth:

- **Delete the word 'perfection' from your vocabulary.**
  You expected only sunshine. But storms are part of the story, too. Both are gifts.
- **Don't run from growth. Run to it.** You're crying because you're being cleansed. You're shedding the darkness the enemy wanted you to keep. Let the light lead you now.

To Do:

- Limit your social media time.
- Journal honestly about how you feel at this moment.
- What do you need to prune to grow?

For every moment you feel broken, find two reasons you're blessed. Here's one to start: **You're alive.** Which means there's still time for God to rewrite your story.

Day 6: You Are an Ambassador for God

When you stop living for yourself, that's when you truly start living.

The root of many of our worries is the belief that we live for ourselves and that we're doing life alone. The enemy feeds us catchy slogans like *YOLO (You Only Live Once)* or *"I was born alone, and I'm going to die alone."* These lies keep us in bondage—and they couldn't be further from the truth.

We were born to live for God. But our human nature often pulls us away from His hand and into self-will. Along that path, we pick up things we were never meant to carry: disease, depression, sorrow, emptiness—even evil. That was never God's intention for us. But because of free will, He lets us write our story.

When we live for ourselves, we settle. But when we live for God, we **soar**. God's plan was never for us to *get by*—it was for us to *glorify*. God wants us to be His **ambassadors**, but many of us are busy playing roles in a life we were never meant to live.

The sooner you realize you were born to give God glory, the sooner you'll start enjoying your life. You're not enjoying life right now because living for yourself is like swimming against the current—while living for God is like floating in His grace.

You don't know what you're supposed to be doing with your life because you've only asked *yourself*—but you've never asked *God*. God wants you to be a **walking church**. A living hymn that makes others sing. A soul that sparks the hunger for Him in others.

People don't have to go to a building to find God—**they should experience Him through you**: through how you treat them, how you make them feel, and how you carry yourself. So ask yourself: **Are you representing God? Or are you just representing yourself?**

Representing yourself is worldly. It leads to selfish, surface-level living. Representing God, however, makes you **worthy of His wealth**—not just material, but eternal. It's selfless living, Spirit-led living. It's choosing to serve instead of being seen.

When you represent God, you function in Spirit—not self. You are moved by what God *needs*, not by what you *want*. And every single day, you have the opportunity to bring someone closer to Him.

Be mindful of that because someone's salvation may depend on what you say. The Word of God should not just be *on* you—it should be *in* you.

You are the walking Word. Embody it.

Scriptures to Meditate On:

2 Corinthians 5:20 (NLT) *"So we are Christ's ambassadors; God is making His appeal through us. We speak for Christ when we plead, 'Come back to God!'"*

Mark 1:17 (NKJV) *"Then Jesus said to them, 'Follow Me, and I will make you become fishers of men."*

How to Be an Ambassador for God:

- **Marry the Spirit. Divorce the flesh.** Living for yourself hasn't gotten you anywhere—I know because it didn't get me anywhere, either. It's time to **discipline your flesh** and function from your **spirit**.

What does that look like?

- Choosing peace when you have every reason to choose war.
- Putting down the liquor and picking up the Bible.

- Honoring your body because you have reverence for God.

The moment you think beyond yourself, your life will begin to bless not just you—but everyone around you.

- **Spread the Gospel.** Share God in your *own unique way*—through blogging, vlogging, podcasting, speaking at work, mentoring, serving in your community, or simply showing up in love.

Ask yourself: *How can my life bring God glory?*

To Do:

Start a fast.

Fasting quiets the flesh and strengthens the spirit. It teaches your body that it doesn't always get what it wants—and that your soul answers to God.

Fasting is a sacred discipline and a necessary one for any Christian who wants to grow. It helps you let go of *yourself* so you can receive *more of Him.*

During this fast, ask God to **empty you of everything that isn't from Him** so that you can be **filled with more of Him.**

Lose yourself—so you can finally be found.

Day 7: You Are a Sacred Space

Merriam-Webster defines a *temple* as "a building for religious practice or a place devoted to a special purpose." The word *sacred* means "dedicated or set apart for the service or worship of a deity."

You are both.

You are a **temple** and a **sacred space**—set apart by God to worship, glorify, and reflect Him. The very essence of your being should be intentional about honoring Him. Because when you know **who you are** and **whose you are**, you speak divinely, walk confidently, and become intentional about what you allow into your temple.

To put it in perspective, imagine yourself as a glass of pure water. Add just one drop of dye and the entire liquid changes color. That's what happens when we allow sin to enter our body, mind, and spirit. One drop of compromise—be it fornication, gluttony, jealousy, envy, or laziness—can contaminate your entire content.

Being a sacred space means being **conscious** of how you spend your time, where you spend it, and with whom. When you recognize that you are sacred, you'll spend more time worshipping God and working on yourself—because you understand your value.

When you know you're sacred:

- The club won't excite you, but sightseeing and soul-searching will.
- You'll stop engaging with people whose energy is tarred with darkness.
- You'll realize that **bad company corrupts good character**.
- The gossip you once joined will become the Gospel you want to share.
- The alcohol you once reached for will be replaced with living water.

Learn to respect yourself as a realm.

Scriptures to Meditate On:

1 Corinthians 3:16 (NLT) *"Don't you realize that all of you together are the temple of God and that the Spirit of God lives in you?"*

1 Corinthians 6:19–20 (NLT) *"Don't you realize that your body is the temple of the Holy Spirit, who lives in you and was given* *to you by God? You do not belong to yourself, for God bought you at a high price. So you must honor God with your body."*

Romans 12:1–2 (ESV) *"I appeal to you, therefore, brothers, by the mercies of God, to present your bodies as a living sacrifice, holy and acceptable to God, which is your spiritual worship. Do not be conformed to this world, but be transformed by the renewal of your mind, that by testing you may discern what is the will of God, what is good and acceptable and perfect."*

How to Operate as a Sacred Space:

- **No sex before marriage.** Our culture glorifies sex, but if you're serious about becoming sacred, abstinence is a must. Sex is a spiritual exchange—and what may feel like pleasure in the moment can leave you carrying someone else's pain. Abstinence keeps your temple clean and your mind clear.

- **Close cancerous chapters.** Say no to new invitations from old places. Not everyone from your past deserves access to your present. If you're reading this book, it's because you're ready to reach your higher self. Reaching that place will require walking away from people, places, and things that keep you tied to the old you.

Being sacred requires separation before elevation.

To Do:

During your time reading this devotional—and even after—be mindful of what you consume. This includes:

- The food you eat.
- The music you listen to.
- The shows you watch.

Your diet isn't just physical. It's also **mental** and **spiritual**.

What you consume influences what you produce. And as a sacred space, you must guard your intake—because your input affects your output.

Day 8: Your Faith Will Turn It in Your Favor

You may have every reason to feel frightened right now, but a warrior doesn't win the war by worrying. A warrior wins the war with worship—thanking God in advance for the victory. A warrior has vision and can see the win before they even prepare to fight. As they fight, it is their *faith* that fuels their hope and makes them heroic.

True victory lies in the ability to focus on faith. When you fix your thoughts on the positive, you create the fuel necessary to stay powered. Life is all about perspective. Having a *God perspective* allows us to enjoy every part of life—whether we're on the hilltop or in the valley. God is with us through both the wins and the wars. You never have to fight alone.

You must speak *life* into your life and over every situation because there is life or death in the power of the tongue. If you have a defeated mindset, you will live a defeated life. But if you walk like a winner—regardless of the cards you're dealt—you will see victory manifest.

Scriptures to Meditate On:

Matthew 6:31–33 (NKJV) *"Therefore do not worry, saying, 'What shall we eat?' or 'What shall we drink?' or 'What shall we wear?' For after all these things, the Gentiles seek. For your heavenly Father knows that you need all these things. But seek first the kingdom of God and His righteousness, and all these things shall be added to you."*

Proverbs 18:21 (NKJV) *"Death and life are in the power of the tongue, and those who love it will eat its fruit."*

Mark 9:23 (NIV) *"'If you can'?" said Jesus. "Everything is possible for one who believes."*

Matthew 17:20 (NIV) *"Truly, I tell you, if you have faith as small as a mustard seed, you can say to this mountain, 'Move from here to there,' and it will move. Nothing will be impossible for you."*

How to Keep Your Faith:

- **Study the Bible.** Going to church is beautiful, but it's not enough to build a strong relationship with God or fortify your foundation. You have to get into the Word. Your pastor can plant a seed, but if you don't go home and water it, the enemy will snatch it away. To increase your faith, increase your time in Scripture. The Word reminds you of God's promises when the enemy tries to plant doubt.

- **Change your environment.** You don't necessarily have to relocate, but it may be time to shift the people around you. Surround yourself with Christian friends who can lift you when you can't lift yourself. Faith-filled friends can remind you of who you are in *God*, not who you are in your *circumstances*. Friends who can pray and praise with you are pivotal to your growth.

To Do:

Write the reference scriptures above on a notecard or in your journal. Read them daily until they are committed to memory. Let them be your spiritual affirmations when your faith starts to waver.

Day 9: You're Built to Endure—Not Just to Survive

Through the Spirit, we have been granted access to an insurmountable amount of strength. Often, we get easily discouraged when faced with challenges because we are leaning on our own understanding and capabilities. But when we surrender our lives and choose to live for God, we gain unlimited access to peace, protection, abundance, salvation—and strength.

As a human, you may not have the strength. But guess who does? God! And all you have to do is ask. Strength will be given to you in Spirit. You lack nothing.

If you depend only on your own strength, you will always feel sunken. But when you shift your perspective to one of prosperity, everything changes. Good thoughts feel good. If you want to make it through a rough time, you must have *ripe* thoughts. Merriam-Webster defines *ripe* as "having mature knowledge, understanding, or judgment." As a Christian, mature knowledge is only found in God, and the highest form of education is found in *studying Him*.

When you study God, your thoughts become seeds. And the more you study His words and His ways, the more you water those seeds. It's in the hard moments of life that you begin to harvest what you've sown. This is why it's important to grow in God—because *that* is where real strength is found when you feel lost.

Scriptures to Meditate On:

Deuteronomy 31:6 (NLT) *"So be strong and courageous! Do not be afraid, and do not panic before them. For the Lord your God will personally go ahead of you. He will neither fail you nor abandon you."*

Psalm 23:1 (NIV) *"The Lord is my shepherd; I shall not lack."*

Isaiah 41:10 (NLT) *"Don't be afraid, for I am with you. Don't be discouraged, for I am your God. I will strengthen you and help you. I will hold you up with my victorious right hand."*

Isaiah 40:29 (NLT) *"He gives power to the weak and strength to the powerless."*

Proverbs 3:5–6 (NIV) *"Trust in the Lord with all your heart and lean not on your own understanding; in all your ways submit to Him, and He will make your paths straight."*

How to Garner Strength:

- **Get out of your funk.** Pick up your bed and walk—not literally, but spiritually. Open the curtains. Clean your house. Buy a new plant. Go to the gym. Read. Write. Do something. If you focus on your fears, you have no time to function in faith.

- **Hurry into healing.** I used to give myself two full weeks to sit in sadness. But as I matured in my Christian walk, I realized I don't need two weeks to be weary. I don't even have time to worry about tomorrow—for tomorrow has enough worries of its own. I learned that if I always look for something to stress over, I will find it. But if I always look for God, I will *also* find Him—and He gives me the optimism I need to remember that everything will be okay if I believe. You may walk through the valley, but you don't have to stay in it.

To Do:

Write down the things you've been through that you never thought you'd survive. Reflect on how you felt *then* and how you felt once you overcame it. This exercise is important because it proves God's point: *You will survive.* Hard times build character. They shape your testimony—and that testimony will bless someone else.

Let me be honest with you: I was once arrested for a DUI and spent 12 long hours in jail. Emphasis on *long.* It was one of the worst experiences of my life—and also one of the most necessary. Prior to that, I had asked God to take away my desire to drink. And guess what? He answered—but not in the way I would've preferred. We can make the request, but we don't get to control God's response.

For a year, I waited anxiously for the outcome of that charge. Would I go to jail for a year? Would I lose my license? Would I be assigned two years of community service like others I'd heard about? I was overwhelmed, anxious, and depressed. But even in the midst of that storm, God was working.

The pain of that season led me deeper into my purpose. That difficult chapter birthed something in me: I became the woman God was trying to get me to become. I no longer have the desire to drink. And though it cost me over $10,000, the lesson was *priceless.*

The charges were dropped. But I picked up something better—a new mindset. God needed me to be fully sober so that I could function at my highest level. The trial was for my good. It taught me things that happy times never could. That's why the Word says, "Count it all joy when you face trials." You will come out better on the other side.

Reflecting on the pain then allows you to appreciate the *harvest* now. Your pain will not be in vain. Strength is waiting to rise from within you.

Day 10: You Have Access to Abundant Peace

In a world filled with war and worry, take time to identify the people, places, and things that bring you peace. Once identified, recognize that these are the things that matter most. Your peace is not optional—it is a priority. If someone or something disrupts your peace and you continue to engage with them or it, you're not protecting your spirit—you're wounding it.

You can't continue to complain about lacking peace if you're the one granting access to the chaos. Peace is a promise from God. It is both accessible and abundant. The solutions to your stress can be simple: if someone's energy feels heavy, spend less time with them. If a place drains you, stop visiting. You are the gatekeeper of your mind. And when your mind is set on God, peace becomes your permanent state.

Instead of focusing on the problem, reposition yourself in the presence of the I Am. God desires for you to live in peace—but He won't force you into it. Do your current actions reflect someone who wants peace? Are you praying for what you won't practice or protect? If you have no peace, it may be because you haven't yet chosen it.

Scriptures to Meditate On:

Isaiah 26:3 (ESV) *"You keep him in perfect peace whose mind is stayed on you, because he trusts in you."*

Philippians 4:6–7 (ESV) *"Do not be anxious about anything, but in everything by prayer and supplication with thanksgiving let your requests be made known to God. And the peace of God, which surpasses all understanding, will guard your hearts and your minds in Christ Jesus."*

John 14:27 (NIV) "Peace I leave with you; my peace I give you. I do not give to you as the world gives. Do not let your hearts be troubled, and do not be afraid."

How to Keep and Create Peace:

- **Start your day with God.** Before checking your phone, checking your calendar, or checking out, open your Bible and check in with the Lord. If you're a parent, imagine your child waking up and walking past you without a word—you'd feel slighted. It's the same with God. Honor Him as the reason you woke up at all. When you begin your day with Him, you're setting the tone for how it will go.

To Do:

For the next few days, choose solitude. Crowds can distract, but becoming requires intention. During your alone time, quiet the noise in your mind and home. Stay in a constant state of prayer. Ask God to enter your atmosphere, steady your heart, and breathe peace into every corner of your life.

Day 11: Self-Care Is the Start, Service Is the Assignment

In a world focused on self-care, remember that after you master loving yourself, you must then love your neighbor. Self-care leads to service.

The self-care industry is currently worth approximately $1.5 trillion—and it's clear that self-sells. People love to focus on themselves, talk about themselves, and live for themselves. There's nothing wrong with prioritizing yourself, but there must be a balance between filling yourself up and pouring yourself out. If everyone only focuses on self, who will focus on serving?

Self-care is not selfish—it's necessary. You cannot give to others what you do not have within yourself. The Bible says, *"Love your neighbor as yourself"*—and loving yourself first is essential.

Many of the relational problems we experience stem from a lack of love for ourselves or from others not loving themselves. Someone who doesn't love themselves will often hate you. Their internal negativity will reject your positivity. The light in you will always irritate the darkness in them. To fix this, everyone must take time to love themselves deeply and fully. And once we master self-love, we must make it our mission to give that same love to others. When we do this, love becomes infectious—just as God intended.

If we could shift from a self-care mindset to a **we-care** mindset, the world would transform rapidly. Don't be blinded by the message that everything has to be about *you*. Everything should be about *us*. If your love cup is full, it's time to share it.

God sent us here to serve each other. You have to figure out what serving looks like for you. For me, serving means writing this book in hopes of helping someone become who and what God has called them to be. For others, serving may be showing up as a chef and preparing meals that make others feel loved and warm. Your way of serving is rooted in your skill set.

Once you discover what that is, do it well—and do it often. You serve yourself when you fulfill the dream. You serve others when you distribute it. God wants us to be selfless in our serving—not consumed by our self-care.

Scriptures to Meditate On:

John 13:34–35 (ESV) *"A new commandment I give to you, that you love one another: just as I have loved you, you also are to* *love one another. By this, all people will know that you are My disciples if you have a love for one another."*

Galatians 5:14 (ESV) *"For the whole law is fulfilled in one word: "You shall love your neighbor as yourself."*

James 2:8 (ESV) *"If you really fulfill the royal law according to the Scripture, "You shall love your neighbor as yourself," you are doing well."*

1 John 4:21 (ESV) *"And this commandment we have from Him: whoever loves God must also love his brother."*

Romans 15:1–2 (ESV) *"We who are strong have an obligation to bear with the failings of the weak and not to please ourselves. Let each of us please his neighbor for his good, to build him up."*

1 Corinthians 10:24 (ESV) *"Let no one seek his own good, but the good of his neighbor."*

How to Love Your Neighbor:

- **Put out what God put in you.** That idea you've been ignoring is meant to serve someone else. The more you delay your divine calling, the more you're missing opportunities to love your neighbor. Someone, somewhere, needs to purchase what you're failing to pursue. Loving your neighbor doesn't always mean your literal neighbor—it's bigger than that. God gave you that follow-through is selfish to us all.

- **Get back in the community.** When was the last time you asked your neighbor for sugar? Most of us go to the store instead. We don't take time to truly get to know one another. I'm guilty of pulling into my garage and closing the door right behind me. But recently, I took the time to get to know one of the moms in my neighborhood—she's from Afghanistan. That one hello and smile led to an incredible friendship. I was introduced to a new culture, beautiful food, and genuine kindness. She called me her sister, and I could've cried.

To Do:

This week, make one new connection. Whether you're at the grocery store, a restaurant, school, or work—talk to someone you've never spoken to before. Speak life into their day. Give them a bit of the love that's overflowing from within you.

Day 12: When You Are Disciplined, You Cannot Be Deterred

Merriam-Webster defines discipline as "training that corrects, molds, or perfects the mental faculties or moral character." It also defines it as "control gained by enforcing obedience or order."

Discipline is one of the most important aspects of the human experience because, without it, we lack the dedication necessary to do the will of the Divine. No successful person has ever lacked discipline—in fact, they mastered it.

A lack of discipline leads to destruction, and that is exactly what the enemy wants: to devour and destroy you.

Discipline can save your life. It shields you from distractions and gives you a clear view of your destiny. When you prioritize discipline, you are showing respect to your future self and your highest self.

Disciplined individuals reach their full potential. Distracted ones shrink from it.

The disciplined succeed because they are committed to their calling. The distracted fall because they are entangled in comfort.

When you commit to discipline, you show reverence to God and honor the path He placed you on.

You can either be disciplined or deterred—but not both.
Which path will you choose?

Scriptures to Meditate On:

Hebrews 12:11 (NIV) *"No discipline seems pleasant at the time but painful. Later on, however, it produces a harvest of righteousness and peace for those who have been trained by it."*

Proverbs 12:1 (NIV) *"Whoever loves discipline loves knowledge, but whoever hates correction is stupid."*

Proverbs 25:28 (NLT) *"A person without self-control is like a city with broken-down walls."*

2 Timothy 1:7 (NLT) *"For God has not given us a spirit of fear and timidity, but of power, love, and self-discipline."*

How to Be Disciplined:

- **Teach yourself to have tunnel vision.** Once you establish a goal, desire, or assignment—lock-in. Don't look to the right or the left. Look forward. Stay focused. Surround yourself with higher-minded and light-minded individuals who feed you spiritually, mentally, and emotionally. As you elevate, you'll crave conversations that carry weight. Tell your ideas to people who can help you manifest them—not to those who let fear blind their belief.

- **Don't let your emotions erase your eagerness to succeed.** Some days, you won't feel like showing up. But discipline is what helps you show up anyway. One step a day is better than no step at all. Focus on the outcome, not the obstacle. The start might feel slow, but your discipline is creating the future you desire. You will win if you work.

To Do:

Wake up one hour earlier than usual and use that time to pursue one of your goals. When the world is still quiet and your mind is calm, connect with your dream. What is the one thing you'd love to do for a living? What brings you so much joy that you'd do it for free? That thing—that dream—deserves your discipline. Before you wake up the kids, answer emails, or get dressed for the day, check in with God—then check in with your purpose. Your dream needs to hear from you, too.

Day 13: Put Down the Vices to Pick Up the Victory

Being distracted is no different than being drunk.
If you live in your vices, you will never have victory.

Driving under the influence impairs your vision and delays your response time. Alcoholic beverages are often called spirits because intoxication suppresses soundness and enhances emotion. It amplifies the nonphysical part of your being—the inner self—often in unhealthy ways.

The French Enlightenment philosopher Jean-Jacques Rousseau once said, "A drunk mind speaks a sober heart." That's because when the mind is sluggish, the heart—usually controlled—can no longer be contained.

Drunkenness has earned its bad reputation, as it should. But distraction? It gets far less attention, even though it's equally dangerous to the human experience. Both drunkenness and distraction fracture your focus—and both can cause accidents on your path to purpose.

A sound mind is a sober mind.
And a sober mind is a clear mind.

As someone who once drank heavily, I learned the hard way that what I thought was clearing my mind was actually clouding it. Overindulging in liquor was just one of many distractions that kept me from the truth.

Many people seek to distract themselves to avoid dealing with their pain. But distraction is dangerous—it takes you off course and keeps you from divine destinations. Instead of listening to the Holy Spirit, you're drinking spirits and engaging with the enemy when you should be sprinting toward God.

Without clarity, you lose sight—and without vision, there is no victory.

Victory requires preparation.
It requires presence.
It requires a clear, focused, sober mind.

People who are victorious are people who prepare. They protect their energy and limit their vices because vices rob them of value.

A soldier does not walk into battle unprotected—they wear armor. But each time you give in to a vice, you remove a layer of that armor, making you vulnerable and unprepared for spiritual war. Vices don't just distract—they weaken.

Scriptures to Meditate On:

Isaiah 5:11 (NLT) *"What sorrow for those who get up early in the morning looking for a drink of alcohol and spend long evenings drinking wine to make themselves flaming drunk. They furnish wine and lovely music at their grand parties—lyre and harp, tambourine and flute—but they never think about the Lord or notice what he is doing."*

Isaiah 5:22 (NLT) *"What sorrow for those who are heroes at drinking wine and boast about all the alcohol they can hold."*

1 Peter 5:8 (ESV) *"Be sober-minded; be watchful. Your adversary, the devil, prowls around like a roaring lion, seeking someone to devour."*

Luke 21:34–36 (NLT) *"Watch out! Don't let your hearts be dulled by carousing and drunkenness and by the worries of this life. Don't let that day catch you unaware like a trap. For that day will come upon everyone living on the earth. Keep alert at* *all times. And pray that you might be strong enough to escape these coming horrors and stand before the Son of Man."*

How to Live a Sober Life:

- **Detox your mind, body, and soul.** Detoxing isn't just about food or fitness—it's about focus. The clearer your mind, the clearer your connection to God. When your mind is decluttered, you can hear Him more clearly and receive the directions you've been praying for. Detoxing improves your concentration, your mood, and your energy. During your transition from being to becoming, detoxing is non-negotiable. You've delayed destiny long enough. This is your wake-up call.

To Do:

Put the vices down so you can pick the victory up. Whether it's drinking, smoking, gossiping, obsessing over love, overworking, or endlessly scrolling—**put it down**. Whatever is pulling you further from peace, from purpose, from your God-given potential, it's time to release it.

Victory requires presence. You can't pursue your purpose if you're sedated by your pain or consumed by distractions.

There's nothing wrong with enjoying life, but the excessiveness is what's damaging your destiny. You don't need a party to find peace. You don't need validation to feel valuable. You need to be *present* so God can *position* you.

This is for you. We need what you are getting ready to produce.

Day 14: Worrying Takes Away from Your Worth

You are valuable—that's why God chose you to be here. You were planned, maybe not by your parents, but most certainly by God. When we worry, we are essentially telling God, *"I know You brought me here, but I don't believe You'll take care of me."* What an insult to Yahweh, the One who can do exceedingly and abundantly more than we ask or imagine. You are deeply cared for, and worrying suggests you do not trust that truth. Worry subtracts from your worth. It adds nothing to your life but anxiety and stress. Thoughts become things—the more you focus on the problem, the bigger it becomes. But here's the good news: you have access to peace through prayer and a relationship with God.

If you're doing your best, let God handle the rest. You may not be where you want to be, but peace can still be found in being still. A busy mind creates mayhem, but a still spirit receives guidance. God wants you to know that worrying is expensive—and not worth the cost. Celebrate your current achievements, whether big or small and trust that everything you're praying for is already yours and waiting for you to catch up.

Scriptures to Meditate On:

Matthew 6:25–27 (NLT) *"That is why I tell you not to worry about everyday life—whether you have enough food and drink or enough clothes to wear. Isn't life more than food and your body more than clothing? Look at the birds. They don't plant, harvest or store food in barns, for your heavenly Father feeds them. And aren't you far more valuable to him than they are? Can all your worries add a single moment to your life?"*

Matthew 6:31–34 (NLT) *"So don't worry about these things, saying, 'What will we eat? What will we drink? What will we wear?' These things dominate the thoughts of unbelievers, but your heavenly Father already knows all your needs. Seek the Kingdom of God above all else, and live righteously, and he will give you everything you need. So don't worry about tomorrow, for tomorrow will bring its own worries. Today's trouble is enough for today."*

Joshua 1:9 (NLT) *"This is my command—be strong and courageous! Do not be afraid or discouraged. For the Lord your God is with you wherever you go."*

How to Stop Worrying:

Let prayer be your first response to a problem. You must learn to fight your battles—not with fear, but on your knees. And once you pray, *leave it there*. Stop picking up what you're trying to hand over to God. He can't step in and fight for you if you don't tag Him in. Aren't you tired of getting beat up?

To Do:

Work more than you worry. Not employment work—but soul work. Go to the gym to strengthen your body. Go to church to strengthen your spirit. Read books that feed your soul. An idle mind has time to worry. A productive mind has no room for it.

Day 15: You Are an Ocean—Stop Seeking Validation from Streams

According to the gospel, we are to be *in* the world but not *of* it. As believers, our aim is not worldly success but heavenly alignment. When we compare ourselves to others, we reduce the divine blueprint God wrote specifically for us. Comparison is a form of spiritual compromise—it makes the monumental feel minimal. But you were not called to shrink. If God is within you, why are you seeking fulfillment outside of you?

The world will always leave you empty. You're looking for food outside when God has already stocked the house. He is the bread of life. He is the living water. And He is enough.

Seeking validation from others is a sign of dehydration. The very people you're waiting on to affirm you cannot quench your thirst—only God can. That's why you must never forget who you are *and* whose you are. You are an *ocean*—you don't need approval from a *stream*. The enemy—the prince of this world— wants you to blend in. But God has called you to stand out.

You are the light in dark spaces, the calm in the storm, the water in a dry land. You are the *salt of the earth.* Don't let the world water you down.

Scriptures to Meditate On:

1 John 2:15–17 (NLT) *"Do not love this world nor the things it offers you, for when you love the world, you do not have the love of the Father in you. For the world offers only a craving for physical pleasure, a craving for everything we see, and pride in our achievements and possessions. These are not from the Father but are from this world. And this world is fading away, along with everything that people crave. But anyone who does what pleases God will live forever."*

1 John 3:1 (NLT) *"See how very much our Father loves us, for he calls us his children, and that is what we are! But the people who belong to this world don't recognize that we are God's children because they don't know him."*

John 15:18–19 (NLT) *"If the world hates you, remember that it hated me first. The world would love you as one of its own if you belonged to it, but you are no longer part of the world. I chose you to come out of the world, so it hates you."*

Romans 12:2 (NLT) *"Don't copy the behavior and customs of this world, but let God transform you into a new person by changing the way you think. Then you will learn to know God's will for you, which is good and pleasing and perfect."*

How to Be in the World but Not of It:

- Refuse to chase trends—pursue truth. Read your Word. Fast. Listen.

- Be set apart. Isolation can lead to elevation. God often speaks the loudest when the world is the quietest.

To Do:

Stop scrolling. If you invested half as much time into your purpose as you do into your timeline, you'd already be walking in your calling. Don't let entertainment rob you of elevation. There's a reason so few people fulfill their destiny—they're too busy watching everyone else live theirs.

Day 16: Because of Your Faith, It Will Happen

You are a powerful magnet, capable of attracting and achieving everything you desire through focused faith. Focused faith is intentionally choosing to believe God's promise—even when you're in pain. It's having negative thoughts, but refusing to accept them—replacing them instead with truth, with light, with God. Focused faith is not optional; it's essential to surviving the human experience.

The only difference between you and someone living their dream is this: they had the courage to step out of their comfort zone and walk into their calling. They chose to believe in themselves. They didn't let failure speak louder than their faith. Faith is the gasoline your car needs to reach destiny. The question is—do you have fuel?

The opposite of faith isn't fear—it's sight. Merriam-Webster defines *sight* as something that is seen, and as a verb, it means to "take aim" or "look carefully in a particular direction." Faith, by definition, is a firm belief in something for which there is no proof. It's unseen. Sight is seen.

And here's why that matters: we choose what we aim at. You can aim your attention at the negative or focus your gaze on God's goodness. Sight can be dangerous when what we see is only a temporary circumstance—but we make it permanent. We make it true. That leaves no space for faith to thrive.

Choosing faith is choosing to reclaim your power. It's choosing peace. It's taking back your sight and looking through the lens of heaven instead of hardship. If you make your faith big, your problems become small.

Scriptures to Meditate On:

2 Corinthians 5:7 (NKJV) *"For we walk by faith, not by sight."*

Matthew 21:22 (NLT) *"You can pray for anything, and if you have faith, you will receive it."*

Luke 1:37 (NKJV) *"For with God, nothing will be impossible."*

How to Have Big Faith:

Being optimistic is not a luxury—it's a necessity for keeping your faith strong. Feed your faith with testimonies. Listen to stories of how God has shown up for others, and let it serve as proof that He will show up for you, too. Focus on what you hear, not what you see. What we see can be deceiving—especially in hard seasons—but we get to choose what we give our attention to.

Call the people who speak life into you. And more importantly, speak life into yourself. Challenge what you see by declaring what you *believe.* Don't speak the problem—speak the promise.

To Do:

Believe. That's it. Believe in what you're praying for. It feels better to think your dreams are going to come true. It feels better to believe everything is working out in your favor—because why wouldn't it? Today, write down what you believe God to do in your life. After reading your Word each day, read that list aloud. Let your faith hear it.

Day 17: You Are a High-Value Being

We live in a society that teaches us that *things* make us valuable. You're considered a high-value individual if you're financially stable, dressed well, and moving among the upper echelon. Sadly, many people believe that tale—and as a result, people with less are often looked down upon for not having more.

But the wealthy aren't winning because they have wisdom or great character. They're winning because they have money. And rarely does anyone stop to ask: *What's going on in their mind?* Money has become the new makeup. Nobody cares what the rich look like underneath anymore.

But hear me: **value transcends wealth.** True richness is rooted in a relationship—specifically, a relationship with God. If you have everything this world can offer but lack God, you truly have nothing. That's not wealth. That's poverty in disguise.

God is the bank. God is the bag. God is the blessing.

Many people are out here learning hard lessons that God never wanted to teach—all because they don't understand where real value lives. The invitation to eternal life is the most priceless gift we've been given. So, if we're going to label anything as "high-

68

value," let it be a character that reflects Christ. Let it be a life lived in reverence. Possessions don't make you rich—purpose does. And while the world may preach wealth, never forget: the *real rich* resides in His realm.

It's also vital to know your identity in God—because if you don't know who you are, the enemy will try to tell you. And he will always try to cheapen your worth. This affects every area of your life.

If you don't know your value in a relationship, you'll settle—accepting less even though your soul is craving more.

If you don't know your value in business, you'll underprice your offerings and overextend yourself trying to prove your worth—when it was already placed in you from the start.

Your value isn't up for debate—it's divine.

Scriptures to Meditate On:

Luke 12:7 (ESV) *"Why, even the hairs of your head are all numbered. Fear not; you are of more value than many sparrows."*

Matthew 6:26 (ESV) *"Look at the birds of the air: they neither sow nor reap nor gather into barns, and yet your heavenly Father feeds them. Are you not of more value than they?"*

1 Timothy 4:8 (ESV) *"For while bodily training is of some value, godliness is of value in every way, as it holds promise for the present life and also for the life to come."*

Hebrews 13:5 (ESV) *"Keep your life free from love of money, and be content with what you have, for He has said, 'I will never leave you nor forsake you.'"*

How to Remember Your Value:

Remember who you were *before* the world tried to tell you who you were supposed to be. Before you saw the magazines. Before you hear the music. Before you went to school or chose a career—who were you? What did you love? What made your soul light up?

Sometimes, we find clarity by revisiting our younger selves. Recently, someone sent me an old video of myself conducting interviews at a music festival in Miami called Jazz in the Gardens. In it, I was interviewing R&B singer Melanie Fiona.

As I watched, I remembered who I used to be. I saw that girl again—radiant, free, fun, and loving before the world tried to make her hard.

In that moment, I honored her. I honored myself.
And I remembered my calling.
I saw my dreams again.

I hope you do, too.

To Do:

Spend the next 10 minutes remembering who you used to be. Not the mistakes—but the dreamer. The one who used to talk boldly about their future. The one who was on fire to fulfill their calling. This is your reminder to bring that fearless version of you back to life.

Are you ready to show up as that person—then, in the now? **Let's go.**

Day 18: You Are Becoming

Change is inevitable. It's not something to run from—it's something to embrace, pursue, and run *toward.* When we get too comfortable in just *being*, we miss the opportunity to *become.*

Becoming is the art of reaching your highest, brightest, most purpose-filled self. A person who has become a light that shines so boldly it inspires others to want to shine, too. But becoming doesn't happen by staying in comfort. You have to get so uncomfortable with *being* that you become determined to do the work to *build* and *blossom.*

I recently heard Myron Golden say, "If you hate your job, don't quit—nothing pushes someone into creating something they love, like a job they hate." That hit me. Sometimes, discomfort is the very thing that pushes us into destiny. If you don't like your life right now, the question is: *What are you going to do about it?*

Becoming looks like perseverance. It looks like endurance. It looks like acceptance. It looks like light. Becoming is character development. Becoming is you.

It's doing the healing internally so you can stop bleeding externally. When you're no longer bleeding, you can finally breathe. And when you can breathe, you can strategize. You can plan. You can *become.*

A person who's satisfied with *being* gives up easily, so growth never happens. But a person who's ready to become? They're okay with crawling until they learn how to walk. Then, they learn how to run. And then—they fly.

Becoming might feel like baby steps, but stepping is still progress. And any step forward is better than standing still.

Scriptures to Meditate On:

Romans 5:3–5 (ESV) *"Not only that, but we rejoice in our sufferings, knowing that suffering produces endurance, and endurance produces character, and character produces hope, and hope does not put us to shame because God's love has been poured into our hearts through the Holy Spirit who has been given to us."*

James 1:2–4 (ESV) *"Count it all joy, my brothers, when you meet trials of various kinds, for you know that the testing of your faith produces steadfastness. And let steadfastness have its* *full effect, that you may be perfect and complete, lacking in nothing."*

James 1:12 (ESV) *"Blessed is the man who remains steadfast under trial, for when he has stood the test, he will receive the crown of life, which God has promised to those who love him."*

How to Become:

Change your habits. Our habits either help us grow or hold us back. If you're not where you want to be in life, it might be time to shift what you're doing daily. It doesn't have to be drastic—start small. Read five pages of a book that grows your mind, your business, or your faith. Small habits lead to big change because what we *repeatedly* do is what shapes who we *become.*

To Do:

Take inventory. Draw a line down a sheet of paper. On the left, write your *negative* habits. On the right, write your *positive* ones. Now ask yourself: *Why am I keeping the negative ones? How can I strengthen the positive ones?*

I'll go first—I used to smoke cigarettes (please don't judge me; this is my safe space). One day I got so disgusted by the habit—

the smell, the damage, the cost—I decided to quit cold turkey. I replaced the habit with running. I knew I couldn't be a smoker and a runner at the same time. One had to go. Thankfully, I haven't smoked in over a year. Glory to God!

Your habits don't define you—but they can definitely *derail* you. Becoming starts with what you repeatedly do. So start doing what pushes you closer to your calling.

Day 19: You Win When You Function More in Spirit Than Self

You are a spiritual being having a human experience, and the only way to truly win in this life is to function more in spirit than in self. The world judges the surface, but God judges the heart. Did you know that God lives in you? Yes, you are walking with divine greatness inside of you. You don't have to find God— you have to acknowledge Him. And the only way to do that is by being present in spirit.

God communicates with us in spirit, which is why it's so important that we silence our surface so we can hear the spirit speak. In this earthly realm, we battle not against flesh and blood but against spirits. We can't always base our experiences on what we *see*, but we must be mindful of what we *feel*. Intuition is not just an inkling to ignore—it's a whisper from God. God is always speaking. Are you listening?

The surface separates us, but the spirit connects us. The surface of our being is where ego and sin live, but a disciplined spirit leads to a fruitful life. If you ever want to remember who you really are, don't look to the mirror—look to your spirit. Your spirit is the truest and purest form of you. When people engage with your spirit, they are enlightened. But when they engage only with your surface, it becomes easier for the ego to be enlarged and the truth of who you are to shrink.

Scriptures to Meditate On:

John 4:24 (ESV) *"God is spirit, and those who worship him must worship in spirit and truth."*

1 Corinthians 12:13 (ESV) *"For in one Spirit, we were all baptized into one body—Jews or Greeks, slaves or free—and all were made to drink of one Spirit."*

Romans 8:9 (ESV) *"You, however, are not in the flesh but in the Spirit, if, in fact, the Spirit of God dwells in you. Anyone who does not have the Spirit of Christ does not belong to him."*

Galatians 5:16 (ESV) *"But I say, walk by the Spirit, and you will not gratify the desires of the flesh."*

1 Peter 2:11 (ESV) *"Beloved, I urge you as sojourners and exiles to abstain from the passions of the flesh, which wage war against your soul."*

How to Function in Spirit:

Stay in a constant state of prayer. The more you pray, the more you're guided. We cannot get through this human experience alone—at least, I know I can't, and I don't want to. Prayer keeps us anchored in purpose and aligned with God. Be intentional about suppressing your surface and calling on your spirit to lead. Always ask yourself: *Would God be pleased with this decision?* That one question will save you from so much unnecessary hardship.

And above all, pay attention to how things *feel*, not just how they *look*. Looks can be deceiving, but those little feels? That's where your wisdom lives. Have you ever been around someone and felt their energy was off? That's not random—that's a revelation. Sometimes, your spirit is telling you to run, and sometimes it's telling you to rest. You'll know the difference if you slow down and listen.

To Do:

Keep God's commandments. The more you focus on keeping His word, the more you dwell in spirit and distance yourself from sin, which is rooted in the flesh. Living in obedience builds discipline, and discipline builds a life God can be proud of.

If you refrain from premarital sex, excessive drinking, holding grudges, gluttony, or any other distractions, you're training your flesh to bow to your spirit. Every time you say no to sin, your spirit gets stronger. And the stronger your spirit becomes, the clearer your calling will be.

Day 20: Just Because You Are in War Doesn't Mean You Won't Win

When we experience difficulty, it's easy to get discouraged. We often focus on the pain of the present instead of the promise of the future. Many people never get to taste the fruit of their labor because they leave the table before God has had time to serve the meal. We run from battles when we should be praying for bravery. Bravery isn't bought—it's built. Soldiers don't go to war expecting defeat; they enter with a mindset of victory, and you should do the same.

No one enjoys war because the fear of loss often screams louder than the blessing of the lesson. The "what if" can paralyze us more than the "why not," but you must choose which voice you'll listen to. When faced with a fight, our instinct is to take flight. But if you flee, you'll eventually find yourself back in the same place—until you learn what God is trying to teach you. Are you ready to grow, or are you going to keep running?

Going into battle and walking into your calling are very similar. Both can be scary. Both require courage. But the real test is whether or not you're willing to try. Try to fight. Try to win. Or even try and fail. Because if you don't try at all, you'll never know what you're truly capable of.

The beautiful thing about life is that even if you lose, you can fight again. If you fail, you learn—and then you try again, this time with more wisdom, more strength, and more perspective. Falling doesn't always mean failure. Sometimes, falling is a necessary step toward rising. Every great leader will tell you— they're thankful for their losses because they prepared them for their wins.

Scriptures to Meditate On:

Deuteronomy 20:1–4 (ESV) *"When you go out to war against your enemies and see horses and chariots and an army larger than your own, you shall not be afraid of them, for the Lord your God is with you, who brought you up out of the land of Egypt. And when you draw near to the battle, the priest shall come forward and speak to the people and shall say to them, 'Hear, O Israel, today you are drawing near for battle against your enemies: let not your heart faint. Do not fear or panic or be in dread of them, for the Lord your God is he who goes with you to fight for you against your enemies, to give you the victory.'"*

Joshua 1:9 (ESV) *"Have I not commanded you? Be strong and courageous. Do not be frightened, and do not be dismayed, for the Lord your God is with you wherever you go."*

Psalm 18:39 (ESV) *"For you equipped me with strength for the battle; you made those who rise against me sink under me."*

Ephesians 6:10–18 (NIV) *"Finally, be strong in the Lord and in his mighty power. Put on the full armor of God so that you can take your stand against the devil's schemes... And pray in the Spirit on all occasions with all kinds of prayers and requests..."*

How to Be a Warrior:

Run toward the battle instead of running from it. Stop asking, "What if I lose?" and start imagining what it will feel like when you win. Problems will come—expect them. Prepare for both the best and worst-case scenarios. But whatever you do, don't live in a place of fear. Walk in faith. You don't come from a place of lack—you come from divine abundance. It's time to access it.

To Do:

Dust off those old ideas you've been too afraid to pursue. What's holding you back from stepping fully into your calling? Write down who you would be if fear weren't in the way. Then, write one small thing you can do to start overcoming that fear.

For example, I have a love-hate relationship with public speaking. I love spreading love and light to an audience—it fills my heart—but I get nervous in the preparation. I tend to overthink it. Lately, I've been saying yes to every speaking opportunity that comes my way—not because I feel ready, but because I know I need to grow. How else will I get better unless I keep showing up? Sometimes, you've got to do it scared until you can do it strong. Embrace the war—that's how you win.

Day 21: You Weren't Called to One Flower—You Were Given a Garden

I used to feel unsupported by the people I loved. I'd pour into those who didn't pour into me and forget about the ones who did. I couldn't understand why some people didn't show up for me like I did for them—until I realized many people aren't even showing up for themselves. They can't see God's vision for my life because they're too clouded to see their own. I had to accept that I don't need support from man when I have the support of God. That shift changed everything.

Focusing all your energy on one relationship can drain you and blind you to the ones that truly matter. Relationships are like a garden—every plant needs water and sunlight. If you only water one, the others will wither. And even that one may die if you overwater it.

Healthy pouring requires wisdom. Too much, and the relationship becomes overwhelmed. Too little, and it shrivels. The key is balance—knowing how much to give, how much to keep, and when to pause. You must also learn to value the water you receive, not just obsess over what you give.

Being mindful of your pour doesn't mean withholding love—it means offering it with purpose. Everyone needs watering, even those you find difficult. If you fixate on one person, you may miss many others God placed in your life to love. If you only notice who's not showing up, you'll miss the ones who are.

Think of love as water—essential and sacred. God doesn't ask us to love in exchange for love. He commands us to love because it reflects Him. It's not about what you receive—it's about who you're becoming.

This matters most when you're walking in your calling. Not everyone will support your dream, and that's okay. Your calling wasn't given to *them*. It was given to *you*. Stop waiting for applause from people who were never meant to understand the assignment. Some of your greatest support will come from strangers. Focus on those who see you and pour into those who truly matter.

Don't hold on to the flower that gives you thorns. Look around—the rest of the garden is blooming.

Scriptures to Meditate On:

John 13:35 (ESV) *"By this, all people will know that you are my disciples if you have a love for one another."*

1 Peter 4:8 (ESV) *"Above all, keep loving one another earnestly since love covers a multitude of sins."*

1 John 4:7–8 (ESV) *"Beloved, let us love one another, for love is from God... Anyone who does not love does not know God because God is love."*

1 Thessalonians 4:9 (ESV) *"You have no need for anyone to write to you, for you yourselves have been taught by God to love one another."*

Galatians 5:14 (ESV) *"For the whole law is fulfilled in one word: "You shall love your neighbor as yourself."*

How to Guard Your Heart from Discouragement:

Love without expectation. When love is given with strings, disappointment follows. Pour into your purpose. Focus on the ones who do show up. Redirect your energy.

Disappointment often stems from expecting others to be like us. Release that. Give freely—and let that be enough.

To Do:

Every time you feel tempted to dwell on who isn't supporting you, take that energy and invest it in your purpose. Enroll in a course. Write the chapter. Update the website. Apply for the grant.

Energy can't be destroyed—but it can be redirected. Use it to water your own growth. Focusing on lack keeps you stuck in being. Purpose moves you into becoming.

Day 22: Rereading the Old Chapters in Your Book Is Only Preventing You from Writing New Ones

The enemy loves when we live in the past because it keeps us stuck—and sick. If he can keep us focused on who we *used* to be, he knows it will prevent us from becoming who God has called us to be. A new chapter is waiting to be written, but you keep rereading the old ones—and that won't change what's already been inked.

Right now, you hold a pencil in the present. Write something new. Stop thinking about the *then* and start living in the *now.* The past is gone. It's only a memory, and reliving it is what's making you miserable. People who dwell in the past become disconnected from the present. They stop living and only *think* about life instead of experiencing it.

The Bible gives us a clear warning. In **Genesis 19:26 (NIV)**, as Lot and his wife were fleeing Sodom and Gomorrah, Lot's wife looked back—and instantly turned into a pillar of salt. She was so fixated on what was burning behind her that she failed to focus on the blessing in front of her. God was pulling her out of destruction, but her longing for the past cost her her life. Let that *not* be you. When God saves you from who you used to be, don't look back. Some backslides you don't come back from.

Living in the past is one of the enemy's favorite tactics. The more distracted you are, the less you focus on your purpose. That's why the moment you commit to your calling, distractions seem to increase—old exes reappear, your phone lights up with notifications, and people call at the wrong time. It's not random. It's strategic.

You can't keep falling for it. A disciplined mind is priceless. The more you learn to ignore what doesn't feed your purpose, the more your creativity and productivity will flow. In this season, you must be focused. Someone is waiting on *you* to move in your calling. Their next step may depend on your first one.

Scriptures to Reflect On:

Genesis 19:26 (ESV) *"But Lot's wife, behind him, looked back, and she became a pillar of salt."*

Isaiah 43:18–19 (ESV) *"Remember not the former things, nor consider the things of old. Behold, I am doing a new thing; now* *it springs forth, do you not perceive it? I will make a way in the wilderness and rivers in the desert."*

2 Corinthians 5:17 (ESV) "*Therefore, if anyone is in Christ, he is a new creation. The old has passed away; behold, the new has come.*"

Luke 9:62 (ESV) "*Jesus said to him, "No one who puts his hand to the plow and looks back is fit for the kingdom of God."*"

Philippians 3:13–14 (NLT) *"No, dear brothers and sisters, I have not achieved it, but I focus on this one thing: Forgetting the past and looking forward to what lies ahead, I press on to reach the end of the race and receive the heavenly prize for which God, through Christ Jesus, is calling us."*

How to Live in the Present:

Start by recognizing how thinking about the past *makes you feel.* Often, it hurts. So if it hurts—if it feels like reopening an old wound—why keep doing it?

Make every effort to focus on thoughts that feel good. Why? Because positive thoughts produce the exact brain chemistry and energy needed to move you forward in your journey. They help you align with your calling. *Thoughts become things*—so ask yourself: what are you creating?

To Do:

The best way to limit distractions is to be intentional. When you sit down to write your book, edit your project, teach, serve, or create—**silence the noise**. Put your phone on Do Not Disturb. Create a schedule and communicate it to your loved ones so they're mindful of your focus time.

Even if a call or message comes in during those sacred hours, remind yourself *it can wait*. Be intentional about how and when you'll work on your calling. What are your "calling hours"?

Mine are from 8 PM to 10 PM. Once my workday ends and my son is settled, that's the time I've committed to being obedient to what God has placed in my hands. Use what He's lent you—wisely.

Day 23: Intuition Is a Whisper from God

While we speak with words, God speaks through the Spirit—and we must learn to discern what we feel. We must become fluent in the language the Holy Spirit speaks.

In *1 Kings 19:11–12* (NIV), God's voice is described as a "gentle whisper." If you're not present in spirit, you'll miss it. That whisper is the nudge in your gut, the unease you feel when you're around the wrong crowd or the tension in unsafe situations. When something feels *off* about a person, place, or decision, that feeling may not be anxiety—it may be your answer. It's a warning, not a welcome.

God is always guiding, but if you ignore the Master, you'll miss the messages. When you dismiss your intuition, you turn God's red flags green. And when you do that, you let the flesh lead in places where God is trying to protect you.

Next time you're questioning your intuition, pay attention to how your body responds. How does your nervous system feel in that place or around that person? Is your spirit calm or in chaos? Quiet your mind. Ask: *Why don't I believe what I feel?* Could it be the unhealed part of you that doesn't trust the truth?

If you feel peace with some and unrest with others, it's not a coincidence. That's God's persistence—His protection. Wisdom is planted in your heart, but you have to recognize the whisper to access its wealth.

This matters deeply as you walk in your calling. God will make things clear—you just have to listen. When you're deciding whether to do business with someone, ask your gut. God may whisper, but your heart will scream if it's a bad decision. And anytime you go against your gut, you'll regret it. Always.

Trust the truth in uneasiness. Trust the truth in frustration. Trust the truth in disengaging. Trust the truth when your spirit says someone isn't right. That's not fiction—it's fact. And ignoring it could cost you more than you're willing to pay. Some people don't come back from dismissing God's whisper.

Your intuition is the invisible friend God gives you on this human journey. Accept its wise counsel.

Scriptures to Meditate On:

Ephesians 1:17 (ESV) "*That the God of our Lord Jesus Christ, the Father of glory, may give you the Spirit of wisdom and of revelation in the knowledge of him.*"

Proverbs 2:6–15 (ESV) "*For the Lord gives wisdom; from his mouth come knowledge and understanding... wisdom will come into your heart, and knowledge will be pleasant to your soul.*"

John 16:13 (ESV) "*When the Spirit of truth comes, he will guide you into all the truth... and he will declare to you the things that are to come.*"

1 Corinthians 2:14 (ESV) "*The natural person does not accept the things of the Spirit of God... they are spiritually discerned.*"

How to Recognize the Spirit Speaking:

If you keep having the same feeling around a person or place, the Spirit is saying something. Have you ever been around someone you called a friend but felt like they weren't truly happy for you? Maybe you sensed jealousy or fakeness? That feeling likely wasn't wrong—your spirit picked up on what their words couldn't hide.

The heart speaks louder than the mouth, but many don't hear it because they're not in tune with the Spirit. When a feeling doesn't leave, it's because it's trying to guide you—whether that means taking action or walking away.

One day, I was at the gym and felt a strong pull to speak and pray with a stranger. I thought I was "tripping," but the thought wouldn't leave. I finally obeyed. After we prayed, he lifted his shirt to reveal a healing gunshot wound. God had nudged me to give him hope—and that moment wasn't random. It was divine. That whisper mattered.

To Do:

On the **left side** of a sheet of paper, write down when you feel anxious or uneasy. Where are you? Who are you with? Does it happen repeatedly in that space or around that person? What do you think is causing this recurring feeling?

Then, on the **right side**, write down what you can do to reduce or remove that discomfort. Maybe it means distancing from certain people, setting new boundaries, or even seeking a new job. Don't ignore the discomfort—it could be holding you back from your next level.

God's whisper is not just to guide you—it's to grow you.

Day 24: Your Path to God Doesn't Have to Be Difficult

Let's be honest—this is a safe space. Most of the difficulty in our lives comes from our own decisions. We walk ourselves into situations and then cry out for God to rescue us. We seek Him in hardship, assuming He must be far away. But God has never left. He's been with us since the beginning.

The truth is, we're guilty of trying to find a God who was never lost. I can admit this has been true for me. I've gone on long, exhausting journeys searching *outwardly* for something that was already *inwardly* available. Have you done the same?

In **Genesis 2:7 (NIV)**, we're reminded that when God created us, He breathed His breath into us. That breath still lives within us. God was always with us—and always will be—if we allow Him in. Life doesn't have to be hard. *Difficulty is a choice.*

Even in the moments when we feel lost, God isn't hiding. He's not waiting to be found—He's waiting for us to become aware. The water was already there when we were thirsty. The word *realize* means to "make real" or to "become aware." My prayer is that you don't have to go through a struggle to *see*. See now.

The path to God doesn't have to include pain. It only requires presence. When you understand that difficulty is often optional, you'll also understand that the road to your calling can be smoother than you think. You were born *able*—just like you were born with God already in you.

You can write the book.

You can start the business.

You can open the daycare.

You can become a life coach.

You can teach, you can lead, you can create.

If you didn't have what it takes, you wouldn't have the idea in the first place.

You can choose difficulty, or you can choose destiny—but you can't have both. When you choose destiny, know that God walks with you. So don't fear. Be bold. Be courageous in your calling.

Scriptures to Meditate On:

Genesis 2:7 (NIV) *"Then the Lord God formed a man from the dust of the ground and breathed into his nostrils the breath of life, and the man became a living being."*

Acts 17:27 (NIV) *"God did this so that they would seek him and perhaps reach out for him and find him, though he is not far from any one of us."*

1 Corinthians 3:16 (NIV) *"Don't you know that you yourselves are God's temple and that God's Spirit dwells in your midst?"*

Deuteronomy 31:6 (NIV) *"Be strong and courageous. Do not be afraid or terrified because of them, for the Lord your God goes with you; he will never leave you nor forsake you."*

How to Make Life Easier:

Stop trying to do it all on your own. Ask God for guidance. When you invite Him to be the center of your life, He becomes your coordinator and your caregiver. The beautiful part of this human experience is—you don't have to navigate it alone. You don't have to guess. Just trust Him.

Your only job? Be obedient. Trust His plan. Stay in faith that His plan will unfold—exactly as it should.

To Do:

Pray more than you worry. Once you've prayed over a situation, surrender it. You no longer have access to it. God can't step in until you *step out.* Write down the areas of your life that feel difficult. What's causing the struggle? Have you truly prayed about it?

Day 25: Reveal. Remove. Replace. Let God Do the Rearranging

I'm proud of you—you are *becoming*. And in your becoming, remember: not everyone can go with you. Many won't want to grow with you. As you rise to new heights, those who once walked beside you on the ground may not be able to breathe at your new elevation. If you try to bring them along, they'll either suffocate or pull you back down—clinging tightly to who you used to be.

Be prepared for this transition. Expect it. Embrace it. If you're losing old friends and making new ones, it's a sign that a shift is happening. You are shedding old skin and connecting with people who appreciate the soul God is developing in you.

As we grow spiritually, it becomes vital to surround ourselves with people walking in the same direction—toward the light. I'm a witness to the "reveal, remove, and replace" prayer. I once asked God to reveal who wasn't in alignment with my spiritual growth, to remove them, and to replace them with people who were.

The right people push you toward purpose. They see the flame God lit in your heart and keep a match for the days when you forget you're already burning with divine fire. The right people don't just *do life* with you—they *do God* with you. They pray *with* you and *for* you. They don't prey *on* you.

The company you keep matters. It's easy to be influenced by what you continually entertain. If you're constantly around people who love the world, you'll slowly forget the Word. As Christians, we're called to love all—but we must also use discernment. There's a difference between being cordial and being close. Every associate is not meant to be a disciple.

Even Jesus had boundaries. He had twelve disciples, but He was only close with three—Peter, James, and John. He often separated Himself from the crowd to be with His inner circle. Your circle shapes your center, which is why you can't allow everyone access. Some people carry spiritual toxicity.

As you walk in your calling, take inventory. Who is an associate? Who is a friend? Who is a mentor? Everyone cannot join the divine conference call God is having with you. Some people must be removed from the group chat—and the Spirit will show you who, just like we discussed on Day 23.

Scriptures to Meditate On:

Psalm 1:1–2 (ESV) "*Blessed is the man who walks not in the counsel of the wicked, nor stands in the way of sinners... but his delight is in the law of the Lord, and on his law he meditates day and night.*"

Proverbs 13:20 (ESV) "*Whoever walks with the wise becomes wise, but the companion of fools will suffer harm.*"

1 Corinthians 15:33 (ESV) "*Do not be deceived: "Bad company ruins good morals.*"

2 Corinthians 6:14 (ESV) "*Do not be unequally yoked with unbelievers. For what partnership has righteousness with lawlessness? Or what fellowship has light with darkness?*"

How to Identify Good Company:

Progressive thinkers don't thrive in conversations rooted in gossip and negativity. If every conversation with a friend or family member drains your spirit or leaves you misaligned— evaluate that connection.

The people you can worship with are the people you can grow with. Go where you can grow. If the people in your life aren't growing, ask yourself—where are they going? If you continue entertaining people who refuse to be enriched, you will never be empowered.

To Do:

Who speaks life into you? Write down their names. What about them makes you feel more grounded, supported, and spiritually alive? Once you've identified these people, reach out and thank them. Let them know how much their presence means to your journey. Acknowledge them—because people like that are rare.

And above all, make sure you are to them what they have been to you.

Day 26: Choose to Inspire in a World That Influences

People used to dream of becoming doctors, lawyers, teachers, and engineers—careers rooted in service. But somewhere along the way, we stopped focusing on *serving* and became obsessed with *receiving*. We now live in a generation of influencers who seek praise and promotion more than purpose.

Individuality has been lost. Everyone looks the same—same hair, same nails, same clothes, same shoes, same surgeons... and sadly, the same sunken spirit. Many who make careers off influencing are unknowingly creating full-time clones based on part-time performance. But the world doesn't need more influencers—it needs *inspiration*. It needs people committed to being disciples. And this is where you come in.

Influence is trendy and fleeting. Inspiration is eternal. Why? Because inspiration isn't rooted in lust—it's rooted in *love*—a love deep enough to want others to become everything God has called them to be.

Influencers often seek to be seen, known and praised. But true inspirations? They die daily to themselves so that God can be seen in them. They don't crave praise—they *offer* it. They don't want to be followed—they want to lead others to Christ.

When you ignite the light in someone else, the flame of God has the opportunity to spread. So, ask yourself honestly: *Do I want to be a star or a servant? Do I want to be an influencer or an inspiration?*

While many chase virality, focus on value. While others seek fame choose fruitfulness. Ask: *How can I serve people with my gift?*

If you can answer that question, you'll not only be successful—you'll be walking in your divine assignment. Don't waste your gift by using it for your glory alone. Use it for God. That's what He intended when He gave it to you.

Being an inspiration means helping people see who they're becoming. Influence, on the other hand, convinces people to *want to be you.* And let's be honest—being *under the influence* has never been a good thing. But rising above it? That's where leadership begins, and inspiration flows.

Influence feeds the ego. Inspiration fuels the calling.

The only person we should be following is Christ—He gave us the blueprint for living. You can't be a fisher of men while trying to be like the very ones you were sent to lead.

Inspire by example. Serve the people God sent you to save. Inspiration leaves a legacy that outlasts applause.

Scriptures to Meditate On:

Matthew 28:19–20 (ESV) *"Go therefore and make disciples of all nations... teaching them to observe all that I have commanded you. And behold, I am with you always, to the end of the age."*

Galatians 2:20 (ESV) *"I have been crucified with Christ. It is no longer I who live, but Christ who lives in me..."*

Matthew 4:18–22 (ESV) *"Follow me, and I will make you fishers of men."... Immediately, they left their nets and followed him."*

How to Be an Inspiration:

Live authentically. People are inspired by *truth* and influenced by *tales*. Walk in your truth. Showing up as your full self in a world starving for individuality will have a deeper impact than you know.

When people see your character, they'll be curious. When they see your consistency, they'll care. Just like the fishermen who became fishers of men, Jesus led with humility—not ego. And that alone inspired many.

Walk fully into who you are. That's where your power lives. And that's how others will find theirs.

To Do:

Free yourself from outcomes and expectations. When walking in your calling, focus on obedience—not applause. It's easy to get discouraged when your business doesn't generate sales or your event has low attendance—but don't let results rob you of your reason.

Make a list of your current projects. Next to each one, write the expectations you had. Then, please write the *reason* you started it in the first place.

Now, move forward and focus on *the reason.*

Influence is result-driven.

Inspiration is reason-driven.

Don't forget your reason.

Day 27: The Wise Will Always Strive to Become Wiser. The Teacher Will Forever Be a Student

The wise teacher understands this truth: they will always remain a student. Learning is a constant, and life becomes stagnant the moment we stop seeking knowledge. No one knows it all—and no one should want to. Discovery is both delightful and divine. God wants us to keep learning, which is why we are continually tested.

Some of us don't pass the test because we're ignoring the training. We run from the trials instead of letting the trials teach us. Wisdom comes from both experience and instruction. And when you're surrounded by a blessed crowd, you'll learn to listen more than you speak.

Studying God is the highest form of education. The more you know Him, the more you begin to understand life on a spiritual level. Allow God to order your steps—because when you're following His instruction, you won't get lost.

But if you're always trying to be the instructor, the teacher, the professor, and the driver, your obsession with control is keeping you disconnected from the source. You're running on your own battery—and it's constantly dying. The real power comes from the Source. Stop depending on your limited supply.

Running from wise counsel leaves the "know-it-all" not knowing anything at all. But those who hunger to learn will continue to live. So, are you ready for God to teach you?

The journey of learning is vital to your becoming. It never ends. Healing doesn't mean you'll never hurt again. Life will always bring more to process and more to grow through. The key is to continually gain new tools—and apply them—so you can live at a higher vibration.

Not only will learning be necessary for your healing, but also for your calling. If God has called you to start a business, you need to stay informed about your industry. If He's called you to lead, you need to grow in wisdom. Stay curious. Stay open. Learn to love learning.

Scriptures to Meditate On:

Proverbs 4:13 (NIV) *"Hold on to instruction; do not let it go; guard it well, for it is your life."*

James 1:19 (NIV) *"Everyone should be quick to listen, slow to speak, and slow to become angry."*

Proverbs 13:20 (NIV) *"Walk with the wise and become wise, for a companion of fools suffers harm."*

Proverbs 9:9 (NIV) *"Instruct the wise, and they will be wiser still; teach the righteous, and they will add to their learning."*

Proverbs 1:5 (NIV) *"Let the wise listen and add to their learning, and let the discerning get guidance."*

How to Be a Student:

Talk less. Listen more.

Many people miss valuable lessons because they're too busy showcasing what they already know. There's a reason God gave us two ears and one mouth. Wisdom listens. Growth listens. Becoming listens.

When you are intentional about learning, you show God that you're also intentional about becoming.

To Do:

- **Step into new environments** and get comfortable being uncomfortable. I try a new cuisine every month, one I'm unfamiliar with, so I can immerse myself in a different culture. I sit alone, talk to the server, and ask questions. It may seem small—but it produces a big shift.

- **Take a new course every quarter** for personal or professional growth.

  Platforms like Udemy offer affordable (even free) options—and many come with certifications.

- **Attend a conference** that piques your interest. Search your city for upcoming events that align with your calling.

- **Talk to your elders.** Ask them, "What were you doing at my age?" The wisdom of our seniors is priceless. They've endured storms you may be facing now. Put your phone down. Spark a conversation with someone seasoned.

Day 28: Sit in Silence with Yourself

There are some people in the world who do not like to be alone. These types of people love big crowds, always have a full social calendar, and are rarely single. They don't know how to be. Relationships become a crutch and a comfort. We all know people like this—they carry baggage they won't unpack, and being around others makes them feel safe. For them, silence is dangerous because their thoughts are too loud. Being around people drowns out the depression.

Take a moment to close your eyes and imagine yourself at the beach. Feel your toes sink into the sand. Breathe deeply. Feel the calm that comes with simply *being*. Give yourself five minutes to soak up this space. It feels good, doesn't it?

Silence is a gift. In a world full of noise, it feels good to be quiet. Sitting in silence with yourself is one of the most beneficial things you can do. It's a form of self-care. It gives you the space to be present—not just with yourself, but with God.

We ask God to answer our prayers and then get frustrated when it feels like He's not responding. The truth is, He *did* respond—we were just too busy to hear Him.

You're making yourself busy, and that busyness is keeping you from your best. It's pointless to be busy if you're not productive, and you can't be productive if you never stop to rest, reset, and reflect. Sitting in silence with yourself is saying, "I am prioritizing my purpose." God can't speak if you don't seek. And being a busybody won't keep you blessed—it'll keep you burdened.

You can't answer your calling if you're not listening to the voice of God. We inhale so much throughout the day—sitting in silence is the *exhale*.

I know it's uncomfortable sometimes. Sitting in silence brings you closer to yourself, and sometimes that's painful. But how else will you hear your heart? Distractions will drown you. Sit. Swim in yourself.

Scriptures to Meditate On:

Psalm 46:10 (NIV) *"He says, 'Be still, and know that I am God; I will be exalted among the nations, I will be exalted in the earth.'"*

Lamentations 3:26 (NIV) *"It is good to wait quietly for the salvation of the Lord."*

How to Be Still:

Be intentional with your time. Stop giving it all away to your friends, your family, and your job. Reclaim your time by making time for *yourself.* And when you make time for yourself, you make time for God.

To Do:

- **Put your phone down.** We are being entertained to death. Life is not on your phone—it's right in front of you. The phone is a distraction that's keeping you from the divine.

- **Wake up earlier than your household.** Give yourself a moment of silence to talk to God. Conversations with Him are the coffee your soul needs.

- **Meditate throughout the day.** If meditation feels hard, remember: it's not about thinking about anything—it's about being intentional about what you're thinking about. The best thing to meditate on is God's Word. Pick one verse for the week and keep your mind fixed on it.

- **Use your PTO.** You work more than you rest—and that's not okay. Even God rested. You should, too. You can't rise

- higher if you're always in a hurry. You can't be balanced if you're always busy.

Take the time.

Day 29: If You Don't Listen to the Screams of Your Heart, Your Dreams Will Turn into Whispers

God has placed a calling in each of us—and that calling rings loudly in our hearts. Many hear the ringing but never answer the phone. Your heart has a voice, and sometimes it *screams*. The scream is that deep, burning desire to do something specific. For some, it's to teach elementary school. For others, it's to paint, build, write, lead, or heal.

Whatever it is, we all have that inner scream.

Some people respond to it. Others ignore it. But here's the truth: if you ignore the scream long enough, it will lose its voice. And if you continue to avoid your calling, God may give it to someone else—someone who is willing to do the work to fulfill it.

Why are you leaving your gift unwrapped?

God gave you that gift so you could offer it to the world—for *His* glory. Not answering the call isn't just procrastination—it's disobedience.

If there's something screaming in your heart, *listen* to it while you still can. What is your heart telling you to do? Sadly, many of us take our gifts for granted and then wonder why we're not blessed with more *presents*. But God isn't going to keep giving gifts to someone who isn't a good steward of what they already have.

You are far more powerful than you give yourself credit for. And chances are, the reason you're not fully pursuing your calling is because you don't believe you can actually achieve it. But if you think you *can't*, you won't. And if you think you *can*, you will.

Why would God put that desire in your heart if you weren't capable of fulfilling it? Why do we each have different dreams? Because we were *designed* for them.

If you truly believe in God, then you must also believe what He said in **Mark 9:23 (NIV):** *"Everything is possible for one who believes."*

God believed in you the day you were born. Why don't you believe in yourself? Listen to the scream in your heart—before it stops speaking to you.

Scriptures to Meditate On:

Ephesians 4:1 (NIV) *"As a prisoner for the Lord, then, I urge you to live a life worthy of the calling you have received."*

Jeremiah 29:11 (NIV) *"For I know the plans I have for you,' declares the Lord, 'plans to prosper you and not to harm you, plans to give you hope and a future.'"*

How to Listen to the Heart:

The heart doesn't lie—but the mind does. You've been talking yourself out of the treasure God placed within you. That treasure was never meant to stay hidden. It was given to you to bless others. The best way to listen to your heart is to stop ignoring it.

Honor it. Respect it. Acknowledge it.

To Do:

Take a sheet of paper.

- On the **left side**, write down everything that comes to heart about your calling.
- On the **right side**, write down all the reasons you haven't pursued it yet.

- In the **middle**, identify when and where you feel most inspired to listen to your heart.

Once you discover the source of your inspiration—*protect it.* Visit that space more often. Stay there.

Inspiration fuels the fire. And if you want to make it to the finish line, you've got to stay lit.

Day 30: Your Habits Have to Align with Your Calling

We can talk about the things we want until we're blue in the face, but if your wants have no work, it's only a wish. The habits you have today will determine the life you live tomorrow. We must learn to take more action and talk less—*this* is what separates the dreamers from the doers.

The doers were once dreamers, too—but they laced up their running shoes. The dreamers sit in the bleachers while the doers get on the track. The things you want out of life want *you* too, but you have to show those things that you love them enough to work for them—just like in any relationship.

So ask yourself: Do your habits align with your assignment?

Being intentional with your habits is how you reach new heights. You can't put in minimal effort and expect maximum results. If you change your habits, you can change your life.

Every day, you should be incorporating your calling into your calendar. Build healthy habits that move you one step closer to manifestation. If you're called to be an author, you should be writing at least three days a week. If you're called to start a church, you can start with a virtual location until you have a physical one. There are no excuses—only execution.

Your habits must align with your goals, and your goals must align with God. Think of your habits as steps: every day, you are either walking *toward* your calling or *away* from it. When you see it this way, your entire life becomes intentional.

When you are intentional, your eyes are fixed on the prize—and the prize is *your purpose*. The goal is to live in your calling. That's the greatest gift any human being can walk in during this life.

Imagine meeting God and hearing Him say, *"Well done, my good and faithful servant,"* because you were obedient to the call. That's the real goal. The life hack to fulfilling your mission is to stay in constant pursuit of purpose. Let it burn in you—until God decides it's time to extinguish your flame.

Too many of us tread lightly with our calling. We think we have time but forget that tomorrow is not promised. Any time not spent pursuing purpose is time wasted—time that God will not give back. Honor your time by using it wisely. Honor God by

showing Him that you're grateful for your calling—*by fulfilling it.*
It is a sin to run aimlessly through life, trying to satisfy the
world while ignoring your call.

Scriptures to Meditate On:

1 Corinthians 9:24–27 (NIV) *"Do you not know that in a race, all
the runners run, but only one gets the prize? Run in such a way
as to get the prize... Therefore, I do not run like someone
running aimlessly... I strike a blow to my body and make it my
slave so that after I have preached to others, I myself will not be
disqualified for the prize."*

James 4:17 (NIV) *"If anyone, then, knows the good they ought
to do and doesn't do it, it is sin for them."*

Ephesians 4:1 (NIV) *"As a prisoner for the Lord, then, I urge you
to live a life worthy of the calling you have received."*

How to Align Your Habits with Your Calling:

Once you recognize your calling and accept that deep knowing
within you, there's no more room for excuses. God is trying to
ignite something in you. Aligning your habits with your calling
starts with valuing yourself. When you value yourself, you
protect your energy—and your calling deserves that same

protection. Alignment also requires prioritization. When your calling becomes a priority, you will naturally begin making decisions that reflect it. Every day, you should be doing something that your calling can benefit from.

Time is not to be wasted binge-watching shows or partying when the purpose is calling. Everything is fine in moderation, but the mission must remain front and center. When the mission leads, the habits follow.

To Do:

Write down what you believe your calling is. Now, start *acknowledging yourself as that.* Get in the habit of identifying with your calling. There is life and death in the power of the tongue. This simple act of calling yourself what God has already declared you to be will raise your vibration and align you with the very thing you're meant to attract.

You don't need permission—you need alignment.

For example, I believe I'm called to be a writer, so I call myself an *author.* Three books in, and I'm just getting started.

How you identify yourself is important. See yourself the way God sees you.

You are called.

Day 31: Don't Let Praise Go to Your Head or Rejection Go to Your Heart

On this calling journey, you will find yourself asking others for advice—and you won't always like their answers. You'll share your dream with people who don't believe, and unintentionally, they'll discourage you. You'll present your vision to the world, and some will love it while others will hate it.

Now is a good time to grow thick skin for your soft heart. Now is a good time to remember: everyone won't see the vision God gave you. And that's okay.

You cannot let praise go to your head or rejection go to your heart. If you do, you'll lose before you ever get the chance to win.

Everything in this world is temporary—even happiness. Embrace every moment—the good, the bad, the beautiful, and the ugly—but don't be easily moved by them. If you get energized by praise, you'll begin to chase it. And when it's missing, you'll feel unworthy. If you're destroyed by rejection, you'll never fly, paralyzed by the fear of being criticized.

Praise and rejection are paralyzing people. Praise inflates the ego and stalls evolution. Some people won't take creative risks because they're afraid they won't get the applause they're used to. For example, you'll notice some artists whose music never changes. They're afraid to grow because they're addicted to approval.

Others are so afraid of rejection that they never even start. Maybe they shared a dream once, and someone laughed instead of celebrating. That rejection sent them back into their shell—and they've been hiding ever since.

Allowing praise to puff you up or rejection to weigh you down can kill your calling before it's ever birthed. Learn to protect your heart and your mind. Everything you do will either build you or break you. Like a nucleus membrane protects what enters and exits the cell, you must guard your inner life. Your calling depends on it.

If people don't support you, stop calling them about your calling. If they reject what you're offering, keep marketing—*the right people will find you.*

The enemy loves it when we get distracted by praise and pain. It keeps us from creating. And we were made in the image of the *Creator*. So create anyway.

Learn this lesson. And learn it fast.

Scriptures to Meditate On:

Romans 12:3 (NIV) *"Do not think of yourself more highly than you ought, but rather think of yourself with sober judgment."*

Proverbs 16:18 (NIV) *"Pride goes before destruction, a haughty spirit before a fall."*

John 15:18 (NIV) *"If the world hates you, keep in mind that it hated me first."*

James 4:6 (NIV) *"God opposes the proud but shows favor to the humble."*

Proverbs 29:5 (NIV) *"Those who flatter their neighbors are spreading nets for their feet."*

Romans 16:18 (NIV) *"With smooth talk and flattery, they deceive the minds of naive people."*

How to Not Be Ruled by Praise or Hindered by Rejection:

When you understand that you were born for a purpose—a seed God planted within you—you won't worry about who refuses to water it or who doesn't want to eat the fruit.

All that matters is this: **God gave you the seed**, and it's *your job* to grow it.

The Bible tells us to be fruitful and multiply. You can't do that if you're caught up in praise or paralyzed by rejection. If you want to be free from both, start by seeing them as *gifts*. Learn to be thankful for praise and rejection alike. Take them at face value— nothing more.

Be thankful. And keep it moving. Because *neither* can pave the way for your purpose.

To Do:

Start complimenting yourself—*daily*. Each morning, look in the mirror and acknowledge everything about you. The shape of your eyes, your nose, your smile, your ears, your eyebrows—*all of it*.

Accept who you are. The more you praise yourself, the less you'll need others to do it for you. Outside recognition is extra—your cup should already be full of the love you pour into yourself.

Day 32: Your Inability to Forgive Is Keeping You from Becoming

It's often said that forgiveness isn't for others—it's for *you*. And I know that to be true. A lack of forgiveness can eat away at your soul like cancer. If you're praying for a new chapter but haven't closed the last one, you're not in the position to receive what's next. Chapters only close through forgiveness. And no matter how much you try to live a new life, the stench of the old one will follow you until you cleanse yourself of it.

When you don't forgive—yourself or others—you stay stuck in the very place you're trying to run from. Unforgiveness makes you run in circles. You think you're being productive, but really, you're being pointless and aimless.

When you carry hurt, you weigh yourself down. It puts cement on your spirit. Forgiveness is freeing. Unforgiveness is a prison. Learn to let go—*instantly and frequently*. Doing so keeps you light, floating instead of frozen.

The truth is, we'll all face things we didn't ask for. Some pain we brought on ourselves and some was inflicted by others. But regardless of the cause, *you get to choose your outcome*. When you choose forgiveness, you choose *yourself.* You choose to be free from something that likely isn't serving you.

Unforgiveness keeps you in bondage. You might think it's protecting you—but really, it's hurting you. It keeps you sick when God is trying to make you well. It keeps you bitter when God is trying to make you whole. The victim storyline doesn't suit you anymore. It's time to change the narrative.

Unforgiveness is heavy. And you can't walk lightly in your calling if you're carrying what's not meant for you. Maybe you haven't lifted your gift because you're too busy holding on to grief—grief that others handed you and grief you gave yourself.

I know this because I've been there. I was once a grief carrier. My first book openly talked about my depression, and as a poet, I lived in it because pain made me feel creative. But now? I want to be creative *without* anxiety, sadness, or depression. I want to be in love—but in love with *God.*

It's not that you don't have a gift. It's that you've been focusing more on your grief than on your grace. Forgiveness is going to take you to a new level.

Let's start today.

Scriptures to Meditate On:

Ephesians 4:32 (NIV) *"Be kind and compassionate to one another, forgiving each other, just as in Christ God forgave you."*

Matthew 6:14–15 (NIV) *"For if you forgive other people when they sin against you, your heavenly Father will also forgive you. But if you do not forgive others their sins, your Father will not forgive your sins."*

Matthew 18:21–22 (NIV) *"Then Peter came to Jesus and asked, 'Lord, how many times shall I forgive my brother or sister who sins against me? Up to seven times?' Jesus answered, 'I tell you, not seven times, but seventy-seven times.'"*

1 John 1:9 (NIV) *"If we confess our sins, he is faithful and just and will forgive us our sins and purify us from all unrighteousness."*

Colossians 3:13 (NIV) *"Bear with each other and forgive one another if any of you has a grievance against someone. Forgive as the Lord forgave you."*

How to Forgive:

Acknowledge what happened. Accept that you can't change the past. What's done is done. Continuing to relive it is draining your present and delaying your future. If you don't accept *what was*, you won't be ready for *what is*—and that's why God hasn't given it to you yet.

Acknowledge. Accept. Accelerate. Move from *then* to *now*.

To Do:

- **Go to therapy.** Talk to a professional about the hurt you've been carrying. Sometimes, speaking to a stranger helps release the sting. You deserve to be heard by someone who will protect your privacy, not gossip about your pain.
- **Be consistent.** Healing won't happen overnight— especially when the pain runs deep. The release takes time. Open yourself slowly. Let the pressure out before you explode.

Allow yourself to be free. Because you deserve it.

Day 33: You Can Eat, but If You Are Not Hungry for God, You Will Never Be Full

We are all hungry for something, and we often try to satisfy that hunger with worldly things—but the world will never make us full, which is why we are often left unsatisfied. We are eating relationship after relationship, friendship after friendship, job after job, city after city—and we are still hungry.

Do you know why we are never full? It's because we are eating things from the convenience store and not from the garden. God is the garden, and He is the only thing that can fill us. God has already gifted us with everything we need to be healthy and whole.

The job will never make you happy because you were meant to start your own business, and until you do that, you will be living below the blessing God wants to give you. Do you know why the relationships never work? It's because you love your partner more than you love God, and God is a jealous God. He cannot bless you with the marriage until you make Him the love of your life.

You know why you're never happy in any city you move to? It's because you are looking for happiness in things that are temporary instead of the truth. You see, we are hungry for the wrong things, and as a result, we starve because we are not being served and saved by the Spirit.

If you learn to eat of the Word and eat of your purpose, you will see your life start to become more fulfilling. I know you may look at the Word—the Bible—and your purpose and think it's too big for you to digest. But what is the best way to eat an elephant? One bite at a time.

Your purpose isn't bigger than you—it was given to you. Therefore, you are the master of it and have been given authority over it from the Maker. You have to be hungry to pursue it.

You don't have to be intimidated by the Bible or think you have to read it in a year. All you have to do is hunger for it, and it will feed you—verse by verse, day by day.

Be intentional about what you hunger for because it will determine what you eat—and as we know, your diet is everything you consume, not just food, but also music, books, television, the company you keep, and essentially everything you entertain.

Only have a diet that brings you closer to the Divine because when you are close to the Divine, He will let you know where there is produce and where there is poison. Right now, many are eating poison and wondering why they are sick. The world will feed you the bad, but God wants you to enjoy the good. Be mindful of what you eat.

Scriptures to Meditate On:

Matthew 5:6 (NIV) *"Blessed are those who hunger and thirst for righteousness, for they will be filled."*

Psalm 63:1 (NIV) *"O God, you are my God, earnestly I seek you; I thirst for you, my whole being longs for you..."*

Psalm 107:9 (NIV) *"For he satisfies the thirsty and fills the hungry with good things."*

John 6:35 (NIV) *"Then Jesus declared, 'I am the bread of life. Whoever comes to me will never go hungry, and whoever believes in me will never be thirsty.'"*

How to identify if you need to change your diet:

You know if you need to change your physical diet based on how your body feels. If you're feeling lethargic, it's very likely that you need more energized foods like fruits and vegetables.

You'll know you need to change your spiritual diet if you're constantly depressed, anxious, easily agitated, and aggravated. You'll know you need a new spiritual diet if you have low-vibrating energy. If someone asks how your day is going and you say, "I'm surviving," you need a new spiritual diet.

It is very important to identify your spiritual diet because you need a proper one in order to pursue your purpose. Many people are not fulfilling their purpose because they simply do not have the fuel to get there.

To Do:

Once you've identified if you need to change your diet, it's time to get the proper "food." Purchase a study Bible so you don't just read to check a box but so you can understand. Knowledge alone is not power—application of knowledge is.

Also, consider fasting from secular music and television. We are being entertained to death. Now is not the time to be distracted—it's time to be fueled.

Check out spiritual leaders like Myron Golden, Phillip A. Mitchell, Jerry Flowers, and Darius Daniels. Fasting is not only turning down the plate—it includes turning down the noise.

Day 34: Use Your Gift to Serve in Obedience to God

Your gift should be used to serve people in obedience to God.

When you are gifted, it can be easy to focus on yourself instead of serving others. Often, when we discover our gifts, our first thought is how we want to use them—not how God wants us to use them. If your gift is being used solely to fulfill your own desires, you are already on the wrong track. It's time to board a new train. God gave you that gift to serve people. Someone, somewhere, needs what you carry. And if your only concern is how it benefits you, you will miss the opportunity to be a blessing to the world.

Now is the time to ask: *How can my gift be used for a purpose?* If you're a great cook, service might look like putting love into every meal. When people eat your food, they feel loved. That same gift could also be used to serve the less fortunate. When you put your heart into whatever you do, people encounter God through your gift. That's the power of purpose. In our creativity, we become extensions of the Creator. When people experience our gifts, they experience Him. Your gift is not about you—it's about giving it away.

Scriptures to Meditate On:

1 Peter 4:10 (NIV) *"Each of you should use whatever gift you have received to serve others as faithful stewards of God's grace in its various forms."*

Colossians 3:23 (NIV) *"Whatever you do, work at it with all your heart, as working for the Lord, not for human masters."*

How to Use Your Gift to Serve:

The best way to understand how your gift can be used in service is to identify how it can help others. For instance, if you're a singer, singing secular music may entertain you, but it doesn't always serve—sometimes, it even influences people toward sin. On the other hand, singing worship music can stir the spirit and point hearts toward God. Ask yourself: *How can my gift help someone?* Find a need, and see how your gift can meet it.

Keep in mind service does not always mean free. Your gift is a service, and people pay for services. Those in need often still expect to pay for what helps them. When your gift is aligned with purpose, abundance can and will flow from it. Someone's problem is waiting for your purpose.

To Do:

On a piece of paper, draw a line down the middle. On the left side, write down your gift. On the right side, list how that gift can help others. Ask yourself: *How can people benefit from my gift?*

Day 35: Garnering Advice from the Wise Will Take You Higher

You cannot share your dreams with people who are convinced life is a nightmare. They will take your light and consume it with their darkness. While it's comfortable to be around like-minded people, it's more impactful to be around people who think *bigger* than you. Seek advice from bright-minded individuals— those whose vision and insight can help you walk more intentionally in your purpose. Scripture reminds us that the wise listen to wise counsel. So ask yourself: *Are the people advising me truly led by wisdom?*

If your ideas aren't producing fruit, it may not be because your seeds are bad—it could be that they're planted in the wrong environment. If you're seeing some growth but struggling to multiply, you might need to surround yourself with people who serve as fertilizer for your faith and your future.

If you're the smartest person in your friend group, it may be time to prune your circle so that you can continue to grow. And if you're always right, consider befriending those who've been wrong—because learning from their mistakes can help you avoid making your own. Seek out wisdom, and wealth will follow—both spiritually and practically.

Scriptures to Meditate On:

Proverbs 12:15 (NIV) *"The way of fools seems right to them, but the wise listen to advice."*

Proverbs 15:22 (NIV) *"Plans fail for lack of counsel, but with many advisers, they succeed."*

How to Find a Tribe That Can Teach:

It's time to evaluate what you're learning from the people around you. Learning doesn't always come in the form of advice—sometimes, it's through observing character. If you have a friend who remains calm in chaotic moments, and you tend to be the opposite, their influence might help you develop that same steadiness. People influence you—that's why it's important to be surrounded by those inspired by God.

Let's do a heart check: *Is your tribe bringing you tribulation or helping you triumph?* If you're not currently surrounded by people who challenge, inspire, and grow you, start connecting with those who are where you hope to be. Find a mentor who can offer wisdom and perspective.

That doesn't mean abandoning your current friends—unless God leads you to—but it does mean making space for new relationships that can sharpen and stretch you. As you elevate, some connections may weigh you down. And when you're climbing, every step matters. There's no turning back now.

To Do:

Make it a goal to attend two networking meetings this month. One great option is **BNI (Business Network International),** where you can introduce yourself, share what you do, and connect with others who might align with your purpose. These types of spaces not only build your confidence in public speaking but also help you scout new partners, gain new friends, and find potential mentors.

Day 36: Let Go So You Can Grow

If you don't let go, you'll never grow. Your inability to say goodbye to the *now* is delaying the blessing in your *next*.

The best version of you is waiting on the other side of your comfort zone. Sadly, many will never meet their ascended self because they've settled into the shell of their current situation, with no hope—or faith—for what's next. Comfort zones keep us bound, block our blessings, and make no room for growth. In order to grow, we have to *go*. We have to move with intention toward our becoming because everything you desire is already desiring you—but you have to walk toward it.

Too many people are sitting still when God has already told them to pick up their bed and walk.

Throughout the Bible, which is our source of truth, we see leaders who had to leave comfort in order to be obedient. Let me be clear—delaying your yes is still disobedience. Abram, Moses, Joshua, and the apostles all had to walk away from the familiar to step into the future. They followed God despite uncertainty, despite feeling unworthy, and despite not knowing every detail of the plan. But here's the beauty: God loves to count on the ones the world counts out.

If Moses hadn't led the Israelites out of Egypt, Joshua wouldn't have led them into Jericho, and they never would've reached the Promised Land. Someone can't finish what you refuse to start. The apostles left their homes to follow Jesus, and because of their obedience, we have the New Testament. Abram left everything he knew to build a legacy. Ruth left her homeland to follow Naomi, and in doing so, she met Boaz—a man who covered, cared for, and honored her after her great loss. Ruth's obedience led to restoration. Leaving what you know is often the first step to becoming who you're called to be.

Les Brown once said, *"The graveyard is the richest place on Earth because it is here that you will find all the hopes and dreams that were never fulfilled, the books that were never written, the songs that were never sung, the inventions that were never shared, the cures that were never discovered—all because someone was too afraid to take that first step, keep with the problem, or carry out their dream."*

Comfort kills. But discomfort? It leads to divine destinations. Instead of running from it, run *toward* it.

The Israelites constantly complained and longed for Egypt because they were more comfortable in slavery than faithful in freedom. What should've taken them 11 days took 40 years—all because of disobedience. Ask yourself: *Are you comfortable in the slavery of your comfort zone?*

Scriptures to Meditate On:

Genesis 12:1 (NIV) *"The Lord had said to Abram, 'Go from your country, your people and your father's household to the land I will show you.'"*

Matthew 14:28-29 (NIV) *"'Lord, if it's you,' Peter replied, 'tell me to come to you on the water.' 'Come,' he said. Then Peter got down out of the boat, walked on the water and came toward Jesus."*

2 Timothy 1:7 (NIV) *"For the Spirit God gave us does not make us timid, but gives us power, love and self-discipline."*

How to Embrace Discomfort:

Growth doesn't feel good. Discomfort is often the soil where transformation grows. But instead of fearing the feeling, try working *through* it.

I always say—if you can change your thinking, you can change your life. What if, instead of running from the tension, you allowed it to build something in you?

Think of someone in the gym: at first, lifting weights causes pain because of the tension placed on the muscles. But over time, that same tension causes growth. The discomfort pays off. When they try on new clothes, they can *see* the results. The same applies to your life—if you endure the stretch, you will see the shift.

Focus on the fruit, not the friction.

To Do:

Start doing what makes you uncomfortable.

- If you're working on a song, record it and share it with your family and friends.
- If you're starting a business, take the next step and file your LLC.
- If you're writing a book, send your draft to a potential publisher for feedback. *TBN even reviews manuscripts for free!*

The point of this "to do" is to take a step—any step. Big or small.

Are you ready to step into the Promised Land? Or are you going to stay in Egypt?

Day 37: Your Assignment Will Be Revealed in Alignment

Your assignment will not be revealed until you are in alignment.

Oxford Languages defines *alignment* as a position of agreement or alliance. *Alliance* is further defined as a state of being joined or associated. But when it comes to God, I'd take it even deeper: alignment isn't just about association—it's about *relationship*.

If we want to walk in our divine assignment, we must first be in alignment with God. God cannot promote us to new positions if we are not in agreement with His will or in a relationship with Him. Just like any human relationship we value, our relationship with God requires intentionality. We must talk to God, spend time with God, return our gifts to God, call on Him, be vulnerable, stay committed, and practice selflessness. Without a relationship with God, we won't be able to hear His voice—let alone understand His will.

If you've been wondering what your assignment is and feel like you're not hearing God clearly, it may be time to examine your alignment. Are you chasing your own passions? Or are you truly seeking to fulfill the purpose God has designed for your life?

Alignment looks different for each of us. For some, it might mean releasing a toxic relationship. For others, it may mean relocating to the city God has been nudging you toward. Whatever it looks like, one truth remains the same—alignment always requires surrender.

You may be praying for clarity about your assignment, but have you been listening long enough to receive the lesson? God isn't hiding from you—you might be hiding from *yourself*, your potential, and, in doing so, from the God within you.

God has already prepared your purpose. But for you to step into it, you must trust His plan and be willing to follow His directions—even when they don't make sense. You don't need to *understand* the plan; you just need to *submit* to it. Alignment is the part you *can* control. You have the power to place yourself in the right environment, around the right people, and in the right mindset to develop your relationship with God.

Once you are in alignment, your assignment will be revealed.

Are you in alignment?

Scriptures to Meditate On:

Proverbs 3:5–6 (KJV) *"Trust in the Lord with all thine heart; and lean not unto thine own understanding. In all thy ways acknowledge him, and he shall direct thy paths."*

Psalm 37:23 (NLT) *"The Lord directs the steps of the godly. He delights in every detail of their lives."*

2 Timothy 1:9 (ESV) *"He saved us and called us to a holy calling, not because of our works but because of his own purpose and grace..."*

Ephesians 2:10 (NIV) *"For we are God's handiwork, created in Christ Jesus to do good works, which God prepared in advance for us To Do."*

How to Get in Alignment with God:

To get in alignment with God, you must first get in *agreement* with Him. That starts by deeply understanding what God says about *you*. When you know what He says, you'll know how to think about yourself.

Oftentimes, we're out of alignment—not because we aren't gifted—but because we're insecure. God did not send you here to be timid. He sent you here to be *timeless*, creating a legacy that outlives you.

See yourself through *God's* lens, not the world's. The world will plant doubt, but God will give you truth. And in order to know His truth, you must study His Word. You can't recognize what you haven't read.

To Do:

Memorize the verses below. Then, begin incorporating them into your daily affirmations and prayers.

- **1 Peter 2:9 (NIV)** *"But you are a chosen people, a royal priesthood, a holy nation, God's special possession, that you may declare the praises of Him who called you out of darkness into His wonderful light."*
- **2 Timothy 1:7 (NKJV)** *"For God has not given us a spirit of fear, but of power and of love and of a sound mind."*
- **Philippians 4:13 (NKJV)** *"I can do all things through Christ who strengthens me."*
- **Psalm 139:14 (NIV)** *"I praise you because I am fearfully and wonderfully made; your works are wonderful, I know that full well."*

- **Romans 8:37 (NIV)** *"No, in all these things, we are more than conquerors through Him who loved us."*
- **Joshua 1:9 (NIV)** *"Have I not commanded you? Be strong and courageous. Do not be afraid; do not be discouraged, for the Lord your God will be with you wherever you go."*
- **Proverbs 3:26 (NIV)** *"For the Lord will be your confidence and will keep your foot from being caught."*
- **Mark 9:23 (NIV)** *"'If you can?' said Jesus. 'Everything is possible for one who believes.'"*

Day 38: Consistency Really Is Key

It's easy to start something—but much harder to keep going.

Sometimes, we stop because the inspiration fades, the motivation dies out, the resources run low, or the support disappears. But it's the *stopping* that delays your destiny. The truth is, everything you desire desires *you*. It's already yours—but you have to catch up with it. If you stop walking toward your wish, you'll never receive what's waiting.

God calls us to have faith, but He also calls us to *work*. You can't just wish for a thing—you have to *work* for it. And in that work, you must be consistent. What you're praying for won't happen overnight. In this microwave generation, we often want things fast—but fast doesn't last. While you're working for what you're wishing for, God is working on *you*. He's developing your character so you can carry what you're called to.

While staying consistent, you *will* get discouraged. You won't always feel inspired or moved—but that's when you remind yourself why you started. Remember the purpose God planted in your heart. Remember the responsibility that comes with obedience to that heart whisper.

The delay is not denial—it's *development*. Doors are being *built* for you so that when the right time comes, you can knock, and they will open.

I always tell myself: *Give God something to bless.* How can God bless a purpose you're not pursuing? Expectation without effort is egregious. Faith is powerful, but it requires your participation.

Why Is Consistency Important? Consistency matters because your effort is a reflection of how seriously you take your purpose. If *you* don't take yourself seriously, why should God—or anyone else?

Honoring yourself isn't just about self-care—it's about *showing up*. When you show up for yourself, you're showing up for your purpose.

Sometimes, we plateau right before we're about to *peak*. We encounter challenges—what I call our *winters*—and we let those winters turn us cold. Instead of recognizing we're in a season, we sink into discouragement and become distant in spirit. But in order to reach your *peak season*, you have to *endure* the winter. You have to walk through it to get to your summer—your breakthrough, your blessing, your profit.

Consistency is the key to getting out of comfort and walking into calling.

Scriptures to Meditate On:

Galatians 6:9 (NIV) *"Let us not become weary in doing good, for at the proper time, we will reap a harvest if we do not give up."*

Luke 16:10 (NLT) *"If you are faithful in little things, you will be faithful in large ones."*

James 1:12 (NIV) *"Blessed is the one who perseveres under trial because, having stood the test, that person will receive the crown of life..."*

Proverbs 4:25–27 (NIV) *"Let your eyes look straight ahead... give careful thought to the paths for your feet and be steadfast in all your ways."*

1 Corinthians 15:58 (NIV) *"Therefore, my dear brothers and sisters, stand firm. Let nothing move you. Always give yourselves fully to the work of the Lord..."*

How to Stay Consistent:

The key to consistency is not focusing on your *feelings* but on your *obedience*. The truth is, you won't always feel like pursuing your purpose—because feelings are fleeting. One day, you'll be on fire, and the next, it'll feel like your flame went out. That's why you must anchor yourself in *meaning*. If you see your calling as meaningful, you'll be more likely to stay faithful to the mission.

To Do:

Reflect on your calling. Identify how it serves others. When you understand how your gift can help someone else, you'll discover its meaning.

Write a paragraph describing *why* your calling is meaningful. Be clear. Be honest. How will your gift serve others? This paragraph will become the foundation of your effort moving forward.

Day 39: Let Go of the Outcome

The what-ifs in life are always louder than the why-nots—and fear can be crippling. People often scare themselves out of starting something because they focus more on the outcome than on obedience.

"What if people don't like it?"

"What if no one supports me?"

"What if my product doesn't sell?"

"What if I have no customers?"

These thoughts push us right back into our comfort zones—because, as I've said before, comfort feels safe. But if you fixate on the outcome, you'll find yourself striving for perfection instead of walking in purpose. And when perfection becomes the goal, purpose becomes imprisoned. Many are sitting on profitable projects—books, ideas, businesses—that are locked away because they don't believe their work is good enough.

And the enemy? He loves that. He loves when you keep in what God called you to put out, because he knows that if you settle, you'll never soar.

Focusing too heavily on the outcome also calls into question the *quality* of your intentions. If all you care about is success, are you truly being of service? Are you doing it for the "likes," or are you doing it to give God the glory in your life?

Because the truth is—obedience *is* the outcome. That's real success. That's what lets you sleep in peace. When you know you're walking in the will of God, you've already won. In a world where many are drifting, choosing to be *anchored* in your assignment is an act of courage.

As you continue stepping out of your comfort zone and into your calling, do what you love because God told you to.

That desire you have? It's not random.
The ability to paint, perform, write, communicate, solve problems, build, or dream with clarity—that's not a coincidence. That's divine design.

You've been gifted something that the world needs to unwrap. But if you're so concerned with how the world will receive your gift, you may never share it. And in doing so, you rob someone of their blessing—and rob yourself of your abundance.

There's only so much you can earn working for someone else. You're helping fulfill someone else's dream while neglecting your own. But the dream God placed in you? It still stands.

Release the results. Trust God with the rest. Focus on the *journey*, not the destination. If you say you have faith, then *act* like it. Do your part—and let God do His.

Outcomes create anxiety. Obedience creates peace. Focus on what you can do *today*. Tomorrow will take care of itself.

When you relinquish your rights to the outcome and surrender your expectations to God, walking in purpose becomes *blissful*.

Scriptures to Meditate On:

Galatians 6:9 (NIV) *"Let us not become weary in doing good, for at the proper time, we will reap a harvest if we do not give up."*

Proverbs 16:3 (NIV) *"Commit to the Lord whatever you do, and He will establish your plans."*

Matthew 6:34 (NIV) *"Therefore, do not worry about tomorrow, for tomorrow will worry about itself. Each day has enough trouble of its own."*

How to Not Focus on the Outcome:

I used to obsess over the outcome of my podcast. I would check how many likes my clips received, how many subscribers I gained, and whether new content led to more followers. But eventually, I realized that focusing so much on the outcome was robbing me of the *joy* I once felt. It started to feel like a job I didn't even want. And when an episode didn't perform the way I expected, I felt discouraged. But when I stopped *looking for disappointment*, that's when I found joy. I was finally able to release my expectations and enjoy the experience.

If you want to let go of the outcome, fall back in love with the gift. Go back to that *initial spark*—the excitement you felt when you first started. Sometimes, we want the applause. But when you shift your mindset and focus on God getting the glory, your effort changes. What you create becomes meaningful, and what you produce becomes *purposeful*.

To Do:

Write down five things you *love* about your gift.

For example: If you're a poet, you might love how your words stir emotion, how you tell stories, how you give new meaning to old things, or how your words offer healing. If you're a doctor, you might love helping people, solving complex problems, promoting natural healing, or volunteering in underserved areas.

The goal of this exercise is to reconnect you with the *core* of why you love using your gift. Because when you can clearly identify the *love*, you'll always be able to return to it—and that will remind you of your *why*, not just the outcome.

Day 40: You Can't Copy Someone Else's Calling

There are many successful people in the world, and if we're being honest, it's easy to look at what they're doing and feel tempted to do the same—hoping it will lead us to the same level of success.

In this social media age, we are more *connected* on the surface than ever before. We constantly see the highlights of others' lives, and that can cause us to question the truth of our *own*.

Let's be clear: people mostly post the pink, not the blue. You're seeing the curated version, not the complete one. Still, we often see someone thriving in their lane and assume that same lane is meant for us. But that's not always the truth. Sometimes, people are successful in what they're doing simply because they are *called* to it. Their obedience brings their abundance.

You can't fulfill someone else's gift. You can't copy someone else's calling. You can try, but it won't fulfill you—because that's not the food God put on *your* plate. Stop eating what you haven't been served.

If God wanted you to do what they're doing, He would have planted that desire in *your* heart.

Many people equate money with success. That's why when we see someone with wealth, we assume they're fulfilled. But we have to shift our perspective. Yes, money helps us live comfortably—but *purpose* defines success.

If you're not fulfilling your purpose, no amount of money will satisfy your spirit. Don't idolize the rich. Don't copy their path. And don't lose yourself trying to live someone else's dream.

You have to make a conscious decision to do *you*. Doing what *you* were called to do is the real wealth. And when you function fully in that space, abundance follows—because God honors alignment.

I'll say this plainly: answering someone else's phone call will cause you to *miss your own message.* I see this all the time. People mimic others while forgetting themselves—and that is an insult to the Big God who created you uniquely. In doing so, we make ourselves *small.*

Scriptures to Meditate On:

Romans 12:6 (NLT) *"In His grace, God has given us different gifts for doing certain things well. So if God has given you the* *ability to prophesy, speak out with as much faith as God has given you."*

1 Corinthians 12:4–6 (NIV) *"There are different kinds of gifts, but the same Spirit distributes them. There are different kinds of service, but the same Lord. There are different kinds of working, but in all of them and in everyone it is the same God at work."*

1 Corinthians 7:17 (NLT) *"Each of you should continue to live in whatever situation the Lord has placed you and remain as you were when God first called you."*

Galatians 6:4–5 (NLT) *"Pay careful attention to your own work, for then you will get the satisfaction of a job well done, and you won't need to compare yourself to anyone else. For we are each responsible for our own conduct."*

Galatians 1:10 (NIV) *"Am I now trying to win the approval of human beings or of God? Or am I trying to please people? If I were still trying to please people, I would not be a servant of Christ."*

How to Stay Aligned with Your Calling:

Be mindful of who—and what—you allow to influence you. Influence can become a drug, and if you're easily influenced, you'll also be easily lost. And once you go too far off track, it's not always easy to find your way back.

To stay aligned with your calling, stay in constant communication with God. Pray over every opportunity, every meeting, every partnership, and every direction you plan to take. If you don't, you may end up following *someone else's* path instead of your own purpose.

What better way to ensure you're following *your* path than by talking to the One who designed it? There is no better way. This is *the only way* to be sure you're headed toward your destiny— and not someone else's dream.

If you're constantly working on a new project, I challenge you to pause. Step away and ask God for clarity. People who are easily swayed often end up copying others out of confusion, not conviction.

Don't join someone else's Ponzi scheme and settle for less. You deserve your *own* destiny, your *own* story, and your happiness and wholeness depend on it.

To Do:

Instead of copying, *congratulate.* The more you celebrate others, the more confident you become in *who you are.* When you honor others, you show strength, not lack. Copying says, "I don't trust what's in me, so I'll replicate what's in someone else." But the beauty of this human experience is that we're all different— and that should be cherished.

Instead of copying, seek *mentorship.* Ask the people you admire how they reached their level of success—and tailor what you learn to fit your own truth.

Always remember: *you are capable.* You don't need to copy anyone else. Success is waiting for *you*—you just have to go and get it. For the next week, make it your mission to celebrate others. Find five people you're proud of and tell them.

This simple practice will build your confidence. Because when you honor others, you're also honoring the greatness within *yourself.*

Biblical Figures Leaving Their Comfort Zones

You've made it to the end of this 40-day journey, and I hope that you've gathered tools, truths, and timely reminders to help you walk out of your comfort zone and into your calling.

I was able to write this book because I have taken the exact same steps I encouraged you to take. I know what it feels like to walk in just a *shell* of myself—minimizing my light to appease the darkness in others. I know what it's like to have my heart whisper to me daily... until that whisper turns into a scream.

The time is *now*. And it is not by chance that you were guided to this book.

There is a deep knowing in you that you've been called to something greater. The world may have pushed you into war with yourself, but now it's time to fight—and it's time to *win*. Show up for yourself in this season and lock in. Distractions cannot be entertained because *someone* is waiting on you to fulfill your assignment.

If only 8% of people fulfill their dreams, ask yourself: Will you be in the 92% who don't—or in the 8% who do?

I know that stepping out of your comfort zone is scary. But staying in your comfort zone is scarier—because it keeps you in a state of *being* and never becoming.

The Bible offers powerful examples of people who wrestled with fear when called to leave the familiar. One of the most known is Moses.

When God called him to free the Israelites, Moses responded with insecurity and doubt: **"Who am I that I should go to Pharaoh and bring the Israelites out of Egypt?"** — *Exodus 3:11 (NIV)*

Later, he protested again: **"Pardon your servant, Lord. I have never been eloquent... I am slow of speech and tongue."** — *Exodus 4:10 (NIV)*

Moses didn't believe he was capable—but God did because God created him. And everything God creates is *good.* God replied: **"Who gave human beings their mouths? Who makes them deaf or mute? Is it not I, the Lord?"** — *Exodus 4:11 (NIV)*

Despite his fears, Moses surrendered. He emptied himself so he could be filled with the Spirit. We often talk ourselves out of the very thing we were meant to do. But like Moses, people won't be rescued until *you* release control and let God lead.

You don't have to be perfect. You just have to be *willing*. Another powerful example is **Ruth**.

After losing her husband, Ruth made the courageous decision to leave her home in Moab and journey with her mother-in-law Naomi to Bethlehem. She gave up comfort, familiarity, and even her god to follow Naomi and her God. That is bold faith.

Ruth's obedience brought her unexpected abundance. She became the wife of Boaz and entered the lineage of King David—and, ultimately, Jesus Christ.

If Ruth had stayed in Moab, her story wouldn't have been as fruitful. Her obedience *led* to her abundance.

We can learn from so many others:

- **Abraham** who left his homeland for a land God would show him.
- **Esther** who left royal privilege and risked her life to save her people.
- The **disciples** who left their homes, families, and occupations to follow Jesus and spread the gospel.

If they hadn't left their comfort zones, many would not have been saved or redeemed. The fulfillment of your calling isn't optional—it's *mandatory.* If you don't do it, God will pass the assignment to someone who will. His mission will be fulfilled. The question is—will *you* be courageous enough to answer the call?

Why not you?

If you can have faith the size of a mustard seed, you can believe that God has already prepared a place for you on the other side. Just like Moses, Ruth, Abraham, Esther, and the disciples—you are not alone. God didn't put that calling in your heart to leave you hanging.

Absolutely not.

A Prayer for Fulfillment

Heavenly Father,

I come to You today with a heart open to hear You and a spirit ready to surrender. I desire to fulfill my life's purpose and walk boldly in the calling You've placed on my life.

Forgive me for the times I ignored Your voice or delayed my obedience. I'm ready for You to be my compass. Order my steps and orchestrate every part of my life so I can live in alignment with Your will.

Align me with the right people—those who will encourage me, sharpen me, and point me back to You. Keep me inspired so I can complete the assignment You created me for.

Lord, I want to function more in my spirit than in myself. And on the days I forget to give You the glory, lovingly convict me and remind me that everything I have is because of You.

I welcome Your correction. Clear my mind, purify my heart, and help me to lead with integrity. I desire to serve You by serving others with the gift You placed in me.

God, I need You. You are my friend, my provider, my peace, my shelter, my source, and my purpose. Without You, I will lose my way—so include Yourself in every part of my life.

Thank You for what You've done, what You're doing now, and what You've already prepared for my future.

Help me release bitterness and unforgiveness. May nothing distract me from my destiny.

Have Your will and way in me—and in this world. May we all rise to fulfill our callings and reflect Your goodness in everything we do.

Thank You, Father. You are a great God.

In Jesus' name, Amen.

Don't Just Walk in the Calling—Keep It

So, you made it out of your comfort zone. You stepped into your calling. But now what?

It's not just about getting there—it's about staying there. It's about protecting the very thing God placed in your hands. Too often, we focus on the journey to our calling and forget that obedience is what keeps us in it.

Let's not forget the story of Saul.

Saul was on a mission to find his father's missing donkeys—wandering, confused, and likely discouraged. Just as he was about to give up, he encountered the prophet Samuel. What Saul didn't know was that he wasn't just about to find donkeys—he was about to find his destiny.

> *"Then Samuel took a flask of oil and poured it on Saul's head and kissed him, saying, 'Has not the Lord anointed you ruler over his inheritance?'* **—1 Samuel 10:1 (NIV)**

Saul was chosen. And because he was chosen, the Spirit of the Lord came upon him in power. At first, Saul was obedient. He listened. He followed. He walked with God. But somewhere along the way, he stopped calling on the One who had called him. Disobedience crept in. Pride took root. And the presence that once empowered him began to fade.

> *"But now your kingdom will not endure; the Lord has sought out a man after his own heart and appointed him ruler of his people because you have not kept the Lord's command."*
> **—1 Samuel 13:14 (NIV)**

> *"Now the Spirit of the Lord had departed from Saul, and an evil spirit from the Lord tormented him."* **—1 Samuel 16:14 (NIV)**

The truth is some people receive their calling and stop seeking the Caller. They get what they prayed for and forget the One who called them. Oh, how quickly we forget God when the bank account is full. Oh, how quickly we forget the valley when we're standing on the mountaintop.

But your relationship with God cannot be seasonal. It must be sustained. Strengthened. Consistent.

Saul had everything he needed to be great—but he forgot about God. And that's all it took to lose what he had been given.

Don't be like Saul.

Be the one who still prays when things are good. Be the one who seeks God not just for the blessing—but to stay aligned with the blesser. Be the man or woman after God's own heart.

Because your calling is not just about walking into it—it's about walking with Him every step of the way.

A Prayer to Keep the Calling

Dear God,

Thank You for revealing my calling to me and allowing me to walk in it. Thank You for trusting me with the gift You placed inside of me. As I give this gift to the world—for others to unwrap, learn from, and be blessed by—I pray that I always remain humble in how I carry it.

Let me never forget that everything I have comes from You, and everything I do is for You. May I always return to You what You have so generously poured into me? Help me to be a faithful steward of my purpose.

I know how easy it is to be led astray by the flesh, to chase applause, approval, or my own understanding. But Lord, may my spirit always speak louder than self. May my devotion to You drown out any distractions that try to detour me from the path You've prepared.

I want to go deeper with You, God. I want to know You more intimately, walk with You more closely, and hear You more clearly. And if ever You see me drifting—if ever I become more distracted than I am devoted—convict my heart. Pull me back into alignment. Correct me with Your love and redirect me with Your grace.

Keep me grounded in You. Keep me desperate for Your presence. And keep me faithful to the call.

In Jesus' name, Amen.

www.ingramcontent.com/pod-product-compliance
Lightning Source LLC
Chambersburg PA
CBHW051151120626
46547CB00012B/1045